2024 FOOTBALL LEGENDS

THIS IS A MORTIMER CHILDREN'S BOOK
Text, design and illustration
© Welbeck Children's Limited 2023
Published in 2023 by Mortimer Children's Limited
An imprint of the Welbeck Publishing Group
Offices in: London - 20 Mortimer Street, London W1T 3JW &
Sydney - Level 17, 207 Kent St, Sydney NSW 2000 Australia
www.welbeckpublishing.com

Design and layout © Welbeck Children's Limited 2023
Text copyright © Welbeck Children's Limited 2023

All statistical data and player heat maps provided by Opta, under license from Stats Perform.

STATS PERFORM

All rights reserved. This book is sold subject to the condition that it may not be reproduced, stored in a retrieval system or transmitted in any form or by any means, electronic, mechanical, photocopying, recording or otherwise without the publisher's prior consent.

DISCLAIMER
All trademarks, brands, company names, team names, registered names, individual names, products, logos and catchphrases used or cited in this book are the property of their respective owners and used in this book for informational and identifying purposes only. This book is a publication of Welbeck Children's Limited and has not been licensed, approved, sponsored, or endorsed by any person or entity.

A catalogue record for this book is available from the British Library.

10 9 8 7 6 5 4 3 2 1
ISBN 978 1 83935 250 8

Printed and bound in Dubai
Author: David Ballheimer
Senior Commissioning Editor: Suhel Ahmed
Design Manager: Matt Drew
Picture research: Paul Langan
Production: Arlene Alexander

All facts and stats are correct as of June 2023

PICTURE CREDITS
The publishers would like to thank the following sources for their kind permission to reproduce the pictures in this book.

GETTY IMAGES: Aitor Alcalde 61; Ion Alcoba/Quality Sport Images 57; Filippo Alfero/Juventus FC 102; Eric Alonso 27; Emilio Andreoli 11, 83, 103, 107T; Gonzalo Arroyo Moreno 48, 76; Matthew Ashton/AMA 47; Marc Atkins 80; Sam Bagnall/AMA 28; Robbie Jay Barratt/AMA 55, 99, 109T; Giuseppe Bellini 17; Berengui/DeFodi Images 8; John Berry 21, 74, 90; Romain Biard/Icon Sport 106B; Shaun Botterill 44; Paolo Bruno 49; Clive Brunskill 13; David S. Bustamante/Soccrates 22, 60, 65; Pedro Castillo/Real Madrid 34; Jean Catuffe 16, 54; James Chance 94; Matteo Ciambelli/NurPhoto 67; Emmanuele Ciancaglini/Ciancaphoto Studio 69; Gareth Copley 106T; Oscar Del Pozo/AFP 111B; Paul Ellis/AFP 85; Julian Finney 38; Stuart Franklin 92; Alex Gottschalk/DeFodi Images 33; Laurence Griffiths 40; Matthias Hangst 73, 77; Alexander Hassenstein 97; Mike Hewitt 59; Mario Hommes/DeFodi Images 51, 79; Catherine Ivill 12; Chloe Knott/Danehouse 43; Roland Krivec/DeFodi Images 30; Maurizio Lagana 111T; Chris Lee/Chelsea FC 82; Sylvain Lefevre 24; Alex Livesey/Danehouse 39, 68, 91; Marco Luzzani 64, 72; Stuart MacFarlane/Arsenal FC 53; Giuseppe Maffia/NurPhoto 56; Manchester City FC 108B; Angel Martinez 26, 62; Matt McNulty/Manchester City FC 20, 35, 66; Aurelien Meunier/PSG 75; Alex Morton 89; Jonathan Moscrop 29; Alex Pantling 41; Ulrik Pedersen/DeFodi Images 15; Valerio Pennicino 108T; Andrew Powell/Liverpool FC 25; Pressinphoto/Icon Sport 45; Quality Sport Images 88; David Ramos 96; Michael Regan 78, 86, 107B; Alessandro Sabattini 93; Christophe Saidi/FEP/Icon Sport 105; Pedro Salado/Quality Sport Images 14; Fran Santiago 71, 87; Oli Scarff/AFP 5; Justin Setterfield 63, 95, 110T; Alexandre Simoes/Borussia Dortmund 18, 37; Diego Souto/Quality Sport Images 50, 98; Christof Stache/AFP 23; Simon Stacpoole/Offside 101; Jack Thomas/WWFC 7; Tottenham Hotspur FC 70; VI Images 81; Mateo Villalba/Quality Sport Images 36, 109B; Visionhaus 9, 19, 31, 42, 46, 52; Darren Walsh/Chelsea FC 10, 110B; George Wood 100

Every effort has been made to acknowledge correctly and contact the source and/or copyright holder of each picture any unintentional errors or omissions will be corrected in future editions of this book.

2024 FOOTBALL LEGENDS

STATS • PROFILES • TOP PLAYERS

MORTIMER

CONTENTS

HOW TO USE THE BOOK 5

DEFENDERS 6
- David Alaba 8
- Trent Alexander-Arnold 9
- César Azpilicueta 10
- Leonardo Bonucci 11
- Rúben Dias 12
- Virgil van Dijk 13
- José Giménez 14
- Joško Gvardiol 15
- Achraf Hakimi 16
- Théo Hernandez 17
- Mats Hummels 18
- Kalidou Koulibaly 19
- Aymeric Laporte 20
- Marquinhos 21
- Nahuel Molina 22
- Benjamin Pavard 23
- Sergio Ramos 24
- Andrew Robertson 25
- Antonio Rüdiger 26
- Stefan Savić 27
- Thiago Silva 28
- Milan Škriniar 29
- Dayot Upamecano 30
- Raphaël Varane 31

MIDFIELDERS 32
- Jude Bellingham 34
- Kevin de Bruyne 35
- Sergio Busquets 36
- Emre Can 37
- Casemiro 38
- Philippe Coutinho 39
- Fabinho 40
- Bruno Fernandes 41
- Enzo Fernández 42
- Roberto Firmino 43
- Jack Grealish 44
- Frenkie De Jong 45
- Jorginho 46
- N'Golo Kante 47
- Toni Kroos 48
- Sergej Milinković-Savić 49
- Luka Modrić 50
- Thomas Müller 51
- Christian Pulisic 52
- Bukayo Saka 53
- Renato Sanches 54
- Marco Verratti 55
- Giorginio Wijnaldum 56
- Axel Witsel 57

FORWARDS 58
- Karim Benzema 60
- Edinson Cavani 61
- Memphis Depay 62
- João Félix 63
- Olivier Giroud 64
- Antoine Griezmann 65
- Erling Haaland 66
- Ciro Immobile 67
- Diogo Jota 68
- Luka Jović 69
- Harry Kane 70
- Robert Lewandowski 71
- Romelu Lukaku 72
- Sadio Mané 73
- Kylian Mbappé 74
- Lionel Messi 75
- Álvaro Morata 76
- Neymar Jr 77
- Marcus Rashford 78
- Marco Reus 79
- Mohamed Salah 80
- Son Heung-Min 81
- Raheem Sterling 82
- Dušan Vlahović 83

GOALKEEPERS 84
- Alisson 86
- Bono 87
- Thibaut Courtois 88
- David De Gea 89
- Gianluigi Donnarumma 90
- Ederson 91
- Péter Gulácsi 92
- Samir Handanović 93
- Hugo Lloris 94
- Emiliano Martinez 95
- Édouard Mendy 96
- Manuel Neuer 97
- Jan Oblak 98
- Jordan Pickford 99
- Nick Pope 100
- Kasper Schmeichel 101
- Wojciech Szczęsny 102
- Marc-André ter Stegen 103

MANAGERS 104
- Carlo Ancelotti 106
- Laurent Blanc
- Antonio Conte 107
- Unai Emery
- Christophe Galtier 108
- Pep Guardiola
- Jürgen Klopp 109
- Julen Lopetegui
- José Mourinho 110
- Stefano Pioli
- Diego Simeone 111
- Thomas Tuchel

HOW TO USE THIS BOOK

Welcome to *Football Legends 2024* — the exciting book packed with the performance stats of today's biggest stars in the world of football! We have chosen more than 100 players and managers from the world's top five leagues: the Bundesliga in Germany, La Liga in Spain, France's Ligue 1, the Italian Serie A and the English Premier League. **The players are either playing in these leagues or have spent the prime years of their careers up until the 22/23 season operating in these top leagues.**

You can use this book to figure out who you think the best performers are or even get together with friends and play a sort of trading-cards game, comparing the performance records of today's finest defenders, midfielders, forwards, goalkeepers and managers.

The types of stats featured for each position vary, as each position performs a specific role on the pitch. For example, a defender's main job is to stop the opposition from scoring, so the stats focus mainly on this part of their game. Likewise, a striker's tackling is not as relevant as their goal or assists tally. What you will find for all the players is the heat map, which shows how much of the pitch a player covers and which areas they focus they play in or, with goalkeepers, whether their strengths lie in the six-yard box or playing as sweeper-keepers who are comfortable all around the penalty area.

The stats span a player's career to date, playing for teams belonging to one of the top five European leagues. The figures have been collected from domestic league and European match appearances only, and exclude data from domestic cup, super cups or international games. This narrow data pool means that the information is instantly comparable so you can decide for yourself who truly deserves to be known as a living legend of the beautiful game.

DEFENDERS

There are different types of defenders. They cover a range of positions and have different skills. The centre-backs are the big defenders in the middle who mark the opposition strikers. Full-backs operate out wide: they are quick, agile and try to stop wide attackers from crossing balls into the box. Wing-backs play out wide, too, in front of the centre-backs, but also make attacking runs when they have the chance. Finally, the sweeper is the spare defender who is positioned behind the centre-half, ready to help the back four deal with any danger.

WHAT DO THESE STATS MEAN?

AERIAL DUELS WON
75%
This is the percentage of headers a defender has won in his own penalty area, to interrupt an opposition attack.

INTERCEPTIONS
This is the number of times a defender has successfully stopped an attack without needing to make a tackle.

BLOCKS
A shot that is intercepted by a defender - preventing his keeper from having to make a save - counts as a block.

KEY PASSES/PASS COMPLETION
A key pass is one that results in an attacking opportunity. Pass completion indicates as a percentage the player's passing accuracy.

CLEARANCES
An attack successfully foiled, either by kicking or heading the ball away from danger, is regarded as a clearance.

TACKLES
This is the number of times a defender has challenged and dispossessed the opposition without committing a foul.

Did you know?

For about 40 years from the late 19th century, the most common formation was 2–3–5. It featured only two defenders (right-back and left-back), while the centre-half played in midfield. There were five forwards.

4

NATIONALITY
Austrian

CURRENT CLUB
Real Madrid

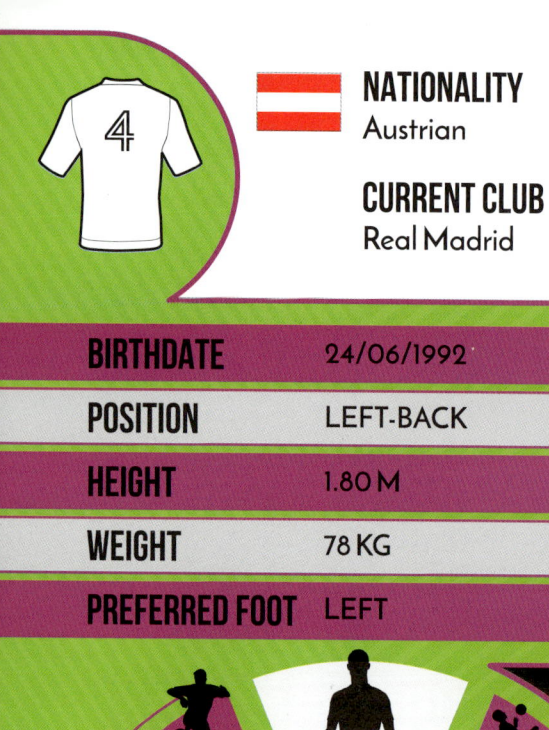

DAVID ALABA

Although his best position is left-back, David Alaba's strength is his versatility. Superb with his positioning and reading of the game, his pace and athleticism also allow him to snuff out attacks before they have begun.

BIRTHDATE	24/06/1992
POSITION	LEFT-BACK
HEIGHT	1.80 M
WEIGHT	78 KG
PREFERRED FOOT	LEFT

- APPEARANCES 465
- INTERCEPTIONS 580
- GOALS 33
- TACKLES 572
- CLEARANCES 632
- KEY PASSES 405
- PENALTIES SCORED 3
- BLOCKS 129
- AERIAL DUELS WON 49%
- PASS COMPLETION 89%

MAJOR CLUB HONOURS

⚽ La Liga: 2022, runner-up 2023 ⚽ Bund'liga: 2010, 2013–21 (x9 all B. Mun.) ⚽ UEFA Champs L.: 2013, 2020 (all B. Mun.), 2022 ⚽ FIFA Club World Cup: 2013, 2020 (all B. Mun.), 2022 ⚽ UEFA Super Cup: 2022 ⚽ Copa del Rey: 2023

INTERNATIONAL HONOURS

⚽ None to date

ACTIVITY AREAS

8

TRENT ALEXANDER-ARNOLD

Counted among the world's best overlapping defenders, Trent Alexander-Arnold plays at right-back or right wing-back. He is fast, tackles superbly and is capable of whipping in accurate crosses that strikers love to feast on!

NATIONALITY English
CURRENT CLUB Liverpool

66

BIRTHDATE	07/10/1998
POSITION	FULL-BACK
HEIGHT	1.75 M
WEIGHT	72 KG
PREFERRED FOOT	RIGHT

- APPEARANCES 250
- INTERCEPTIONS 318
- BLOCKS 34
- AERIAL DUELS WON 37%
- PASS COMPLETION 78%
- PENALTIES SCORED 0
- GOALS 14
- KEY PASSES 497
- CLEARANCES 361
- TACKLES 418

MAJOR CLUB HONOURS
- Premier League: 2020
- UEFA Champions League: 2019
- UEFA Champions League: runner-up 2018, runner-up 2022
- FIFA Club World Cup: 2019
- FA Cup 2022

INTERNATIONAL HONOURS
- UEFA Nations League: third place 2019

ACTIVITY AREAS

9

28

NATIONALITY
Spanish

CURRENT CLUB
Chelsea

CÉSAR AZPILICUETA

Right-back César Azpilicueta is a natural leader, who can play anywhere on the pitch. He is excellent at using his positional sense to snuff out danger and frequently starts counter-attacks with a great right foot.

BIRTHDATE	28/08/1989
POSITION	FULL-BACK
HEIGHT	1.78 M
WEIGHT	76 KG
PREFERRED FOOT	RIGHT

- APPEARANCES: 588
- BLOCKS: 201
- INTERCEPTIONS: 1077
- AERIAL DUELS WON: 58%
- PASS COMPLETION: 82%
- PENALTIES SCORED: 0
- GOALS: 15
- KEY PASSES: 408
- TACKLES: 1543
- CLEARANCES: 1823

MAJOR CLUB HONOURS
- Premier League: 2015, 2017
- UEFA Champions League: 2021
- UEFA Europa League: 2013, 2019
- FIFA Club World Cup: 2021, runner-up 2012
- UEFA Super Cup: 2021
- FA Cup: 2018, 2021, runner-up 2022

INTERNATIONAL HONOURS
- UEFA Nations League: runner-up 2021
- FIFA Confederations Cup: runner-up 2013

ACTIVITY AREAS

10

LEONARDO BONUCCI

Italy's captain since 2022, Leonardo Bonucci is a strong and experienced centre-back with exceptional ball skills. He is superb at breaking up play and launching attacks with long passes. What's more, he poses a goal threat from set pieces.

NATIONALITY Italian

CURRENT CLUB Juventus

19

BIRTHDATE	01/05/1987
POSITION	CENTRAL
HEIGHT	1.90 M
WEIGHT	85 KG
PREFERRED FOOT	RIGHT

APPEARANCES 538
BLOCKS 337
INTERCEPTIONS 887
AERIAL DUELS WON 54%
PASS COMPLETION 87%
PENALTIES SCORED 3
GOALS 34
KEY PASSES 157
TACKLES 608
CLEARANCES 2177

MAJOR CLUB HONOURS
- Serie A: 2006 (Inter Milan), 2012, 2013, 2014, 2015, 2016, 2017, 2019, 2020
- Coppa Italia: 2015, 2016, 2017, 2021

INTERNATIONAL HONOURS
- UEFA European Championship: 2020-runner-up 2012
- FIFA Confederations Cup: third place 2013
- UEFA Nations League: third place 2021, third place 2023

ACTIVITY AREAS

11

3

NATIONALITY
Portuguese

CURRENT CLUB
Manchester City

RÚBEN DIAS

Rúben Dias plays mainly on the left side of central defence, but is comfortable anywhere along the back line. He excels at winning challenges in the air and on the ground, making interceptions and delivering great passes with both feet.

BIRTHDATE	14/05/1997
POSITION	CENTRAL
HEIGHT	1.86 M
WEIGHT	76 KG
PREFERRED FOOT	RIGHT

BLOCKS 79
APPEARANCES 139
INTERCEPTIONS 126
AERIAL DUELS WON 58%
PASS COMPLETION 92%
PENALTIES SCORED 0
GOALS 6
KEY PASSES 33
TACKLES 158
CLEARANCES 365

MAJOR CLUB HONOURS
⚽ Premier League: 2021, 2022, 2023 ⚽ UEFA Champions League: runner-up 2021, 2023 ⚽ Portuguese Premier Liga: 2019 (Benfica) ⚽ FA Cup: 2023

INTERNATIONAL HONOURS
⚽ UEFA Nations League: 2019

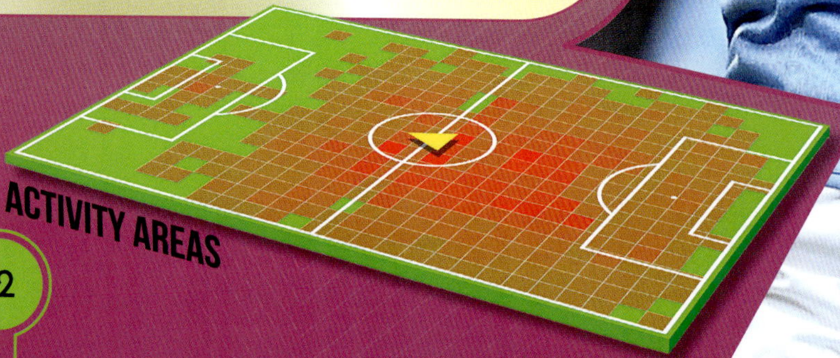

ACTIVITY AREAS

12

VIRGIL VAN DIJK

Virgil van Dijk has returned to the form he showed before his 2020 knee injury. Good with either foot, he is a great tackler, a superb leader, wins headers in both penalty boxes and reads the game excellently.

NATIONALITY Dutch

CURRENT CLUB Liverpool

4

BIRTHDATE	20/06/1991
POSITION	CENTRAL
HEIGHT	1.95 M
WEIGHT	92 KG
PREFERRED FOOT	RIGHT

- APPEARANCES 291
- INTERCEPTIONS 449
- GOALS 24
- TACKLES 281
- CLEARANCES 1481
- KEY PASSES 71
- PENALTIES SCORED 0
- BLOCKS 139
- AERIAL DUELS WON 74%
- PASS COMPLETION 88%

MAJOR CLUB HONOURS
⚽ Premier League: 2020 ⚽ Scottish Premiership: 2014, 2015 (Celtic) ⚽ UEFA Champions League: 2019, runner-up 2018, runner-up 2022 ⚽ FIFA Club World Cup: 2019 ⚽ FA Cup: 2022

INTERNATIONAL HONOURS
⚽ UEFA Nations League: runner-up 2019

ACTIVITY AREAS

NATIONALITY	Uruguayan
CURRENT CLUB	Atlético Madrid

JOSÉ GIMÉNEZ

The Uruguayan is a tough-tackling centre-back who is quick off the mark and difficult to knock off the ball. He made his international debut when he was just 19 and has also thrived at club level since joining Atlético Madrid in 2013.

BIRTHDATE	20/01/1995
POSITION	CENTRAL
HEIGHT	1.85 M
WEIGHT	77 KG
PREFERRED FOOT	RIGHT

- BLOCKS: 154
- APPEARANCES: 258
- INTERCEPTIONS: 423
- AERIAL DUELS WON: 66%
- PASS COMPLETION: 83%
- PENALTIES SCORED: 0
- GOALS: 9
- KEY PASSES: 51
- TACKLES: 390
- CLEARANCES: 1163

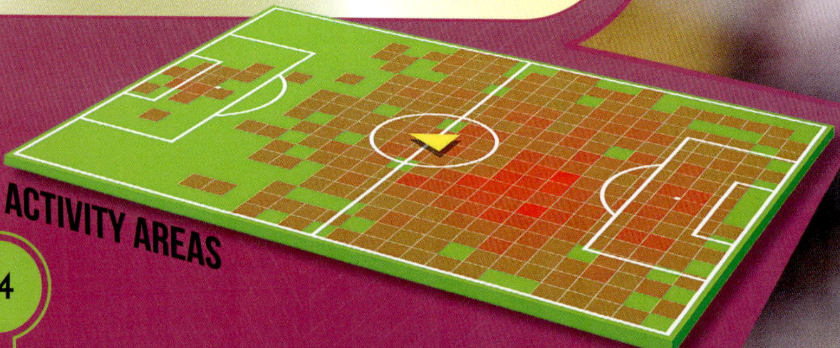

MAJOR CLUB HONOURS
- La Liga: 2014, 2021
- UEFA Europa League: 2018
- UEFA Super Cup: 2018
- UEFA Champions League: runner-up 2014, 2016

INTERNATIONAL HONOURS
- FIFA U-20 World Cup: runner-up 2013
- China Cup: 2018, 2019

ACTIVITY AREAS

JOŠKO GVARDIOL

Twenty-one-year-old Joško Gvardiol has emerged as one of the bright lights in the Bundesliga. His ability to defend in one-on-one situations, play the ball out of the back and pick out the right pass make him a model modern-day centre-half.

NATIONALITY Croatian

CURRENT CLUB RB Leipzig

32

BIRTHDATE	23/01/2002
POSITION	CENTRAL
HEIGHT	1.85 M
WEIGHT	80 KG
PREFERRED FOOT	LEFT

- APPEARANCES 87
- BLOCKS 38
- INTERCEPTIONS 126
- PENALTIES SCORED 0
- AERIAL DUELS WON 58%
- PASS COMPLETION 86%
- GOALS 6
- KEY PASSES 35
- CLEARANCES 192
- TACKLES 110

MAJOR CLUB HONOURS
⚽ DFB Pokal: 2022, 2023

INTERNATIONAL HONOURS
⚽ FIFA World Cup: third place 2022

ACTIVITY AREAS

15

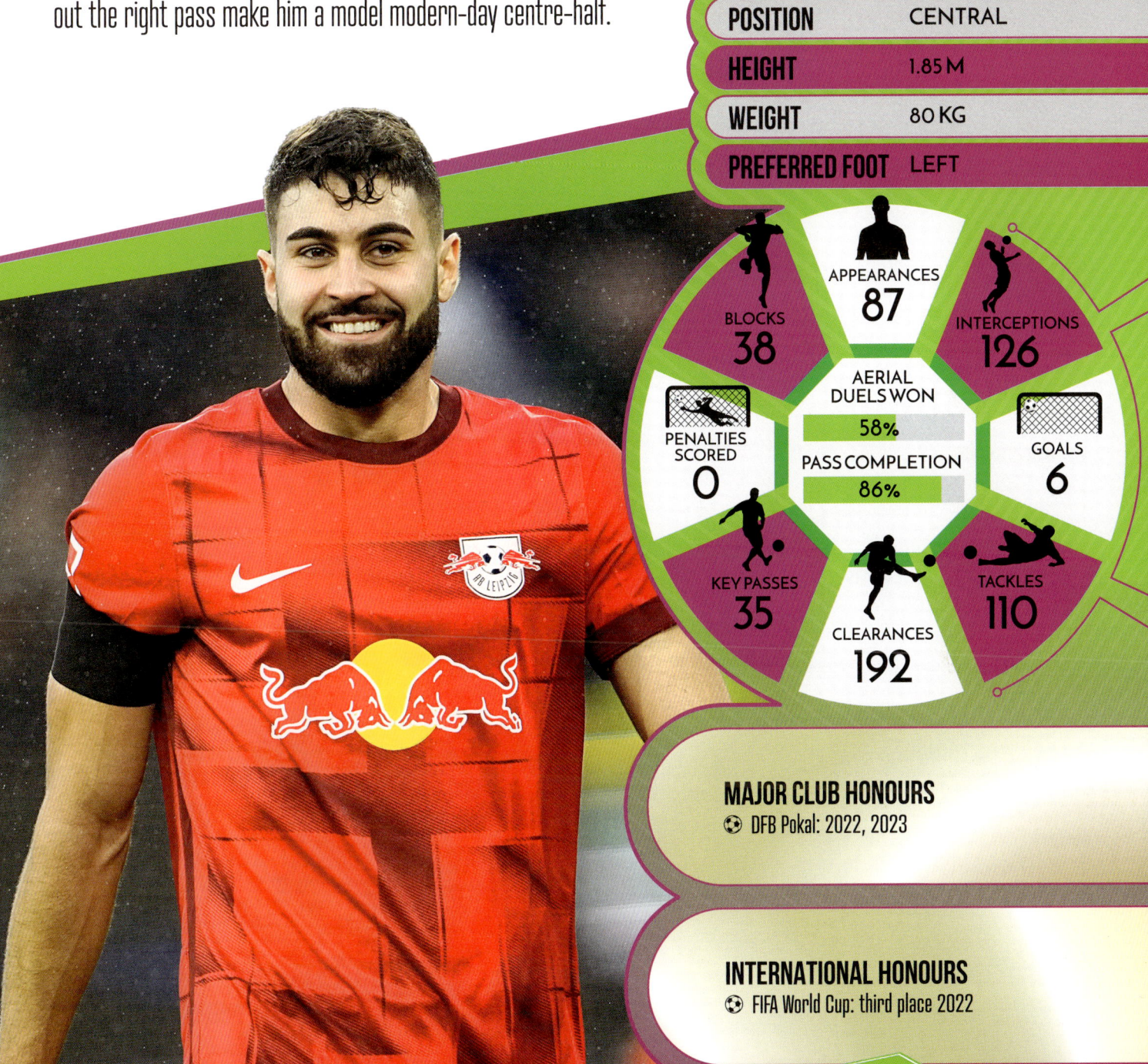

NATIONALITY
Moroccan

CURRENT CLUB
Paris Saint-Germain

ACHRAF HAKIMI

Born in Spain to Moroccan parents, Ashraf Hakimi has played and enjoyed success at some of Europe's top clubs. Known for his blistering pace and keen attacking instincts, he can play as a midfielder or wing-back, and can even score and create goals.

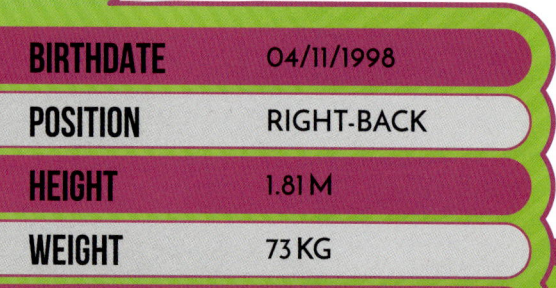

BIRTHDATE	04/11/1998
POSITION	RIGHT-BACK
HEIGHT	1.81 M
WEIGHT	73 KG
PREFERRED FOOT	RIGHT

- APPEARANCES 196
- INTERCEPTIONS 167
- GOALS 29
- TACKLES 361
- CLEARANCES 157
- KEY PASSES 186
- PENALTIES SCORED 0
- BLOCKS 20
- AERIAL DUELS WON 42%
- PASS COMPLETION 87%

MAJOR CLUB HONOURS
- Ligue 1: 2022, 2023
- Serie A: 2021 (Inter Milan)
- UEFA Champions League: 2018 (R. Madrid)
- FIFA World Club Cup: 2017 (R. Madrid)

INTERNATIONAL HONOURS
- None to date

ACTIVITY AREAS

16

THEO HERNÁNDEZ

Known more for his attacking qualities than his defensive work, Theo Hernández (younger brother of Lucas) is a footballer that is blessed with great pace, can dribble rapidly with the ball at his feet, and possesses the capability to get into goalscoring positions. He has become a fan favourite at AC Milan.

NATIONALITY French

CURRENT CLUB AC Milan

19

BIRTHDATE	06/10/1997
POSITION	LEFT-BACK
HEIGHT	1.84 M
WEIGHT	81 KG
PREFERRED FOOT	LEFT

- BLOCKS 45
- APPEARANCES 225
- INTERCEPTIONS 231
- PENALTIES SCORED 3
- AERIAL DUELS WON 64%
- PASS COMPLETION 83%
- GOALS 25
- KEY PASSES 246
- CLEARANCES 297
- TACKLES 384

MAJOR CLUB HONOURS
- Serie A: 2022
- UEFA Champions League 2017 (R. Madrid)
- FIFA World Club Cup: 2017 (R. Madrid)
- UEFA Super Cup 2017 (R. Madrid)

INTERNATIONAL HONOURS
- FIFA World Cup: runner-up 2022
- UEFA Nations League: 2021

ACTIVITY AREAS

15

NATIONALITY	German
CURRENT CLUB	Borussia Dortmund

MATS HUMMELS

The German is regarded as one of the best ball-playing defenders on the planet. Hummels can physically tussle with the strongest of forwards, but it is his ability to stride forward and set up attacks with his fine passing that sets him apart.

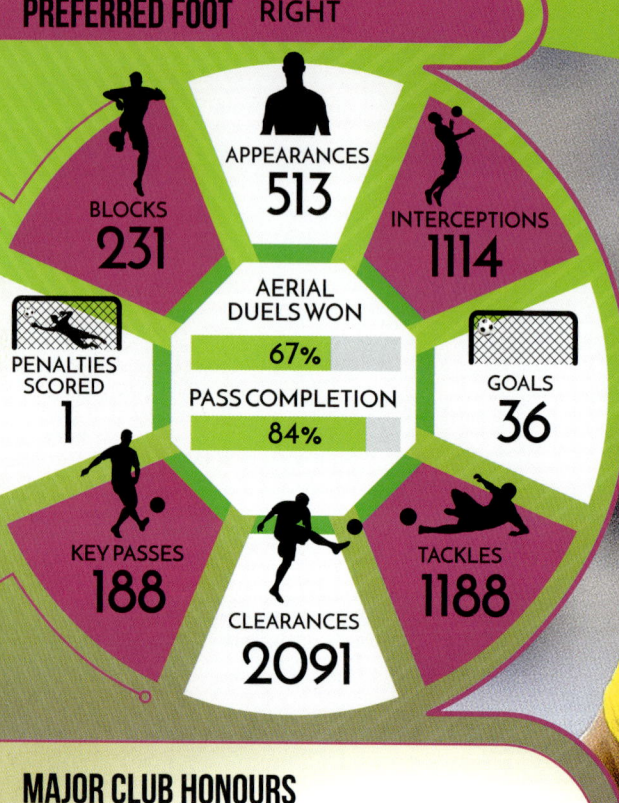

BIRTHDATE	16/12/1988
POSITION	CENTRAL
HEIGHT	1.91 M
WEIGHT	94 KG
PREFERRED FOOT	RIGHT

- APPEARANCES 513
- BLOCKS 231
- INTERCEPTIONS 1114
- AERIAL DUELS WON 67%
- PASS COMPLETION 84%
- PENALTIES SCORED 1
- GOALS 36
- KEY PASSES 188
- TACKLES 1188
- CLEARANCES 2091

MAJOR CLUB HONOURS
- Bundesliga: 2011, 2012, 2017 (B. Mun), 2018 (B. Munich), 2019 (B. Munich), runner-up 2023
- DFB-Pokal: 2012, 2019 (B. Mun), 2021
- UEFA Champions League: runner-up 2013

INTERNATIONAL HONOURS
- FIFA World Cup: 2014

ACTIVITY AREAS

18

KALIDOU KOULIBALY

Kalidou Koulibaly is an aggressive centre-back, perfect for his side's high-pressing game. Extremely fast, he is capable of sprinting back to cover even if the opposition play the ball over the top or in behind his team's high defensive line.

NATIONALITY Senegalese

CURRENT CLUB Chelsea

26

BIRTHDATE	20/06/1991
POSITION	CENTRAL
HEIGHT	1.86 M
WEIGHT	89 KG
PREFERRED FOOT	RIGHT

- APPEARANCES 340
- BLOCKS 271
- INTERCEPTIONS 557
- AERIAL DUELS WON 56%
- PASS COMPLETION 88%
- PENALTIES SCORED 0
- GOALS 15
- KEY PASSES 95
- CLEARANCES 1204
- TACKLES 662

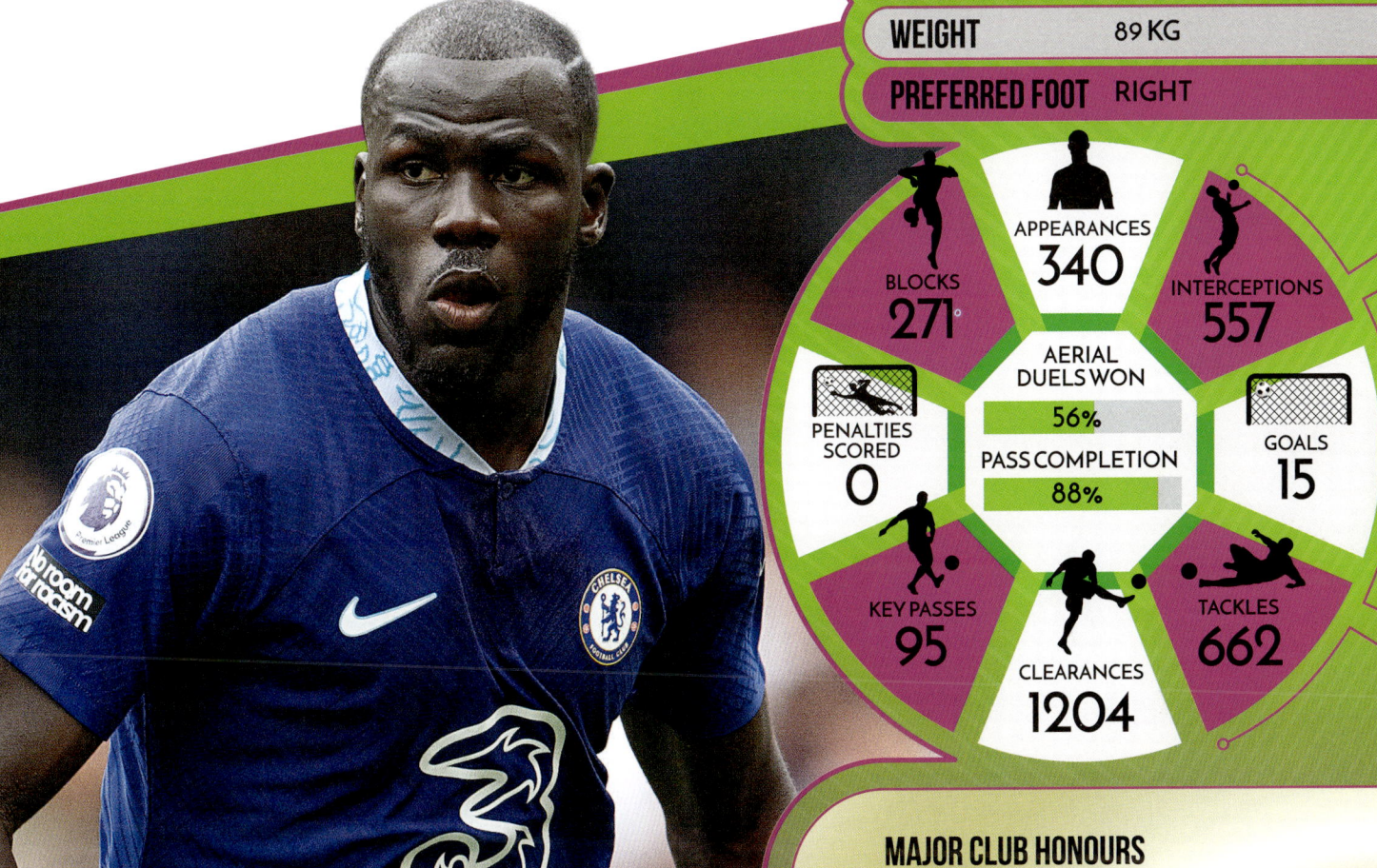

MAJOR CLUB HONOURS
- Belgian Cup: 2013 (Genk)
- Coppa Italia: 2020 (Napoli)

INTERNATIONAL HONOURS
- Africa Cup of Nations: 2021, runner-up 2019

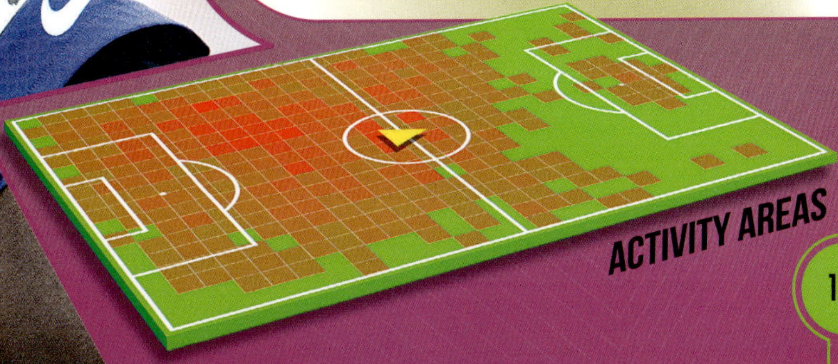

ACTIVITY AREAS

14

🇪🇸 **NATIONALITY**
Spanish

CURRENT CLUB
Manchester City

AYMERIC LAPORTE

Aymeric Laporte has become one of Europe's best central defenders. Very strong, he is powerful in the tackle, excellent in the air and a good organiser at the back. Laporte can also start attacks with his precise passing out of defence.

BIRTHDATE	27/05/1994
POSITION	CENTRAL
HEIGHT	1.89 M
WEIGHT	86 KG
PREFERRED FOOT	LEFT

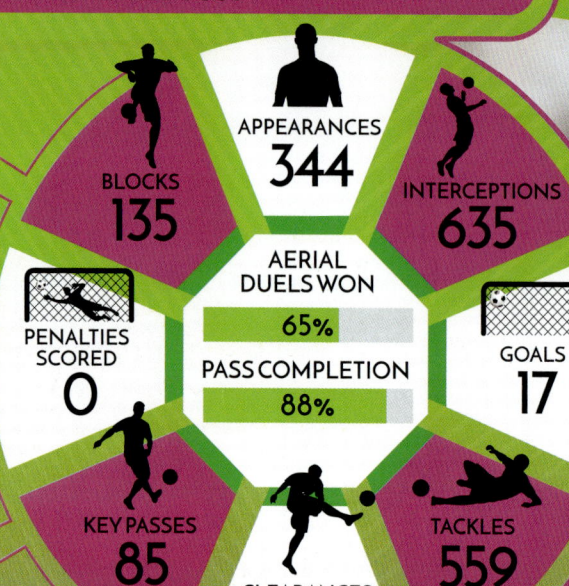

- APPEARANCES 344
- INTERCEPTIONS 635
- AERIAL DUELS WON 65%
- PASS COMPLETION 88%
- GOALS 17
- TACKLES 559
- CLEARANCES 1213
- KEY PASSES 85
- PENALTIES SCORED 0
- BLOCKS 135

MAJOR CLUB HONOURS
- Premier League: 2018, 2019, 2021, 2022, 2023
- UEFA Champions League: runner-up 2021, 2023
- FA Cup: 2019, 2023

INTERNATIONAL HONOURS
- UEFA Nations League: runner-up 2021, 2023
- UEFA European U-19 Championship: runner-up 2013 (France)

ACTIVITY AREAS

20

MARQUINHOS

Marquinhos is a clever defender. He may not be a powerhouse like many of today's top-class centre-backs, but has the speed, agility and intelligence to mark the quickest forwards, plus he can be very effective going forward.

NATIONALITY Brazilian

CURRENT CLUB Paris Saint-Germain

5

BIRTHDATE	14/05/1994
POSITION	CENTRAL
HEIGHT	1.83 M
WEIGHT	75 KG
PREFERRED FOOT	RIGHT

- APPEARANCES: 376
- BLOCKS: 231
- INTERCEPTIONS: 502
- PENALTIES SCORED: 0
- AERIAL DUELS WON: 58%
- PASS COMPLETION: 93%
- GOALS: 33
- KEY PASSES: 76
- CLEARANCES: 1299
- TACKLES: 574

MAJOR CLUB HONOURS

⚽ Ligue 1: 2014, 2015, 2016, 2018, 2019, 2020, 2022, 2023 ⚽ UEFA Champions League: runner-up 2020 ⚽ Coupe de France: 2015, 2016, 2017, 2018, 2020, 2021

INTERNATIONAL HONOURS

⚽ Copa América: 2019, runner-up 2021
⚽ Olympic Games: 2016

ACTIVITY AREAS

16

| NATIONALITY | Argentinian |
| CURRENT CLUB | Atlético Madrid |

NAHUEL MOLINA

Nahuel Molina has worked hard to become a dominant force on the right flank. Very quick, with fine positional sense and good tackling technique, he is also comfortable with the ball at his feet and a tremendous passer in attacking situations.

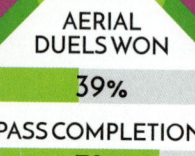

BIRTHDATE	06/04/1998
POSITION	RIGHT-BACK
HEIGHT	1.75 M
WEIGHT	70 KG
PREFERRED FOOT	RIGHT

- APPEARANCES: 103
- BLOCKS: 15
- INTERCEPTIONS: 62
- AERIAL DUELS WON: 39%
- PASS COMPLETION: 78%
- PENALTIES SCORED: 0
- GOALS: 13
- KEY PASSES: 106
- TACKLES: 143
- CLEARANCES: 122

MAJOR CLUB HONOURS
- None to date

INTERNATIONAL HONOURS
- FIFA World Cup: 2022
- Copa América: 2021

ACTIVITY AREAS

22

BENJAMIN PAVARD

Benjamin Pavard has matured into a technically brilliant defender. He has the ability to time his tackle perfectly and shut down opposing players in possession of the ball. He can also move the ball down one or two lines of defence with a single pass.

NATIONALITY French

CURRENT CLUB Bayern Munich

5

BIRTHDATE	28/03/1996
POSITION	CENTRAL
HEIGHT	1.86 M
WEIGHT	76 KG
PREFERRED FOOT	RIGHT

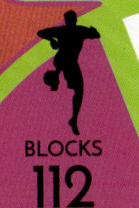

APPEARANCES 229
BLOCKS 112
INTERCEPTIONS 396
PENALTIES SCORED 0
AERIAL DUELS WON 61%
PASS COMPLETION 87%
GOALS 11
KEY PASSES 110
CLEARANCES 688
TACKLES 332

MAJOR CLUB HONOURS
⚽ Bundesliga: 2020, 2021, 2022, 2023
⚽ UEFA Champions League: 2020 ⚽ UEFA Super Cup: 2020
⚽ FIFA Club World Cup: 2020 ⚽ DFB-Pokal: 2020

INTERNATIONAL HONOURS
⚽ FIFA World Cup: 2018, runner-up 2022
⚽ UEFA Nations League: 2021

ACTIVITY AREAS

23

4*
*At Paris Saint-Germain

NATIONALITY
Spanish

CURRENT CLUB
TBC

SERGIO RAMOS

Very quick at anticipating danger, Sergio Ramos is a fine tackler with an excellent positional sense. Not only is he a skilled defender and great team leader, but is also known for regularly scoring important goals for his team.

BIRTHDATE	30/03/1986
POSITION	CENTRAL
HEIGHT	1.84 M
WEIGHT	82 KG
PREFERRED FOOT	RIGHT

- BLOCKS: 319
- APPEARANCES: 696
- INTERCEPTIONS: 1482
- AERIAL DUELS WON: 67%
- PASS COMPLETION: 88%
- PENALTIES SCORED: 18
- GOALS: 94
- KEY PASSES: 289
- TACKLES: 1373
- CLEARANCES: 2804

MAJOR CLUB HONOURS
- Ligue 1: 2022, 2023 (all PSG)
- La Liga: 2007-08, 2012, 2017, 2020 (all R. Mad.)
- UEFA Champions League: 2014, 2016, 2017, 2018 (all R. Mad.)
- UEFA Super Cup: 2014, 2016, 2017 (all R. Mad.)
- FIFA Club World Cup: 2014, 2016-18 (all R. Mad.)

INTERNATIONAL HONOURS
- FIFA World Cup: 2010
- UEFA European Championship: 2008, 2012
- FIFA Confederations Cup: third place 2009, runner-up 2013

ACTIVITY AREAS

24

ANDREW ROBERTSON

In a short space of time, Andrew Robertson has become one of the world's best leftsided defenders. He is fast, an excellent tackler and reader of the game, plus his ability to hare down the flank, complete neat one-twos and whip over dangerous crosses makes him an asset in attack.

NATIONALITY
Scottish

CURRENT CLUB
Liverpool

26

BIRTHDATE	11/03/1994
POSITION	LEFT-BACK
HEIGHT	1.78 M
WEIGHT	64 KG
PREFERRED FOOT	LEFT

APPEARANCES **303**
BLOCKS **58**
INTERCEPTIONS **290**
AERIAL DUELS WON **52%**
PENALTIES SCORED **0**
PASS COMPLETION **83%**
GOALS **9**
KEY PASSES **413**
CLEARANCES **526**
TACKLES **462**

MAJOR CLUB HONOURS
- Premier League: 2020
- UEFA Champions League: 2019
- FIFA World Club Cup: 2019
- UEFA Super Cup: 2019
- FA Cup: 2022

INTERNATIONAL HONOURS
- None to date

ACTIVITY AREAS

22

NATIONALITY
German

CURRENT CLUB
Real Madrid

ANTONIO RÜDIGER

Antonio Rüdiger has become a dominant defender all along the back line, winning tackles with his strength and dominating the penalty area with his heading ability. He is also an excellent passer, reads the game well and leads by example.

BIRTHDATE	03/03/1993
POSITION	CENTRAL
HEIGHT	1.90 M
WEIGHT	85 KG
PREFERRED FOOT	RIGHT

- BLOCKS: 126
- APPEARANCES: 345
- INTERCEPTIONS: 363
- PENALTIES SCORED: 0
- AERIAL DUELS WON: 59%
- PASS COMPLETION: 87%
- GOALS: 16
- KEY PASSES: 81
- TACKLES: 470
- CLEARANCES: 1161

MAJOR CLUB HONOURS
- UEFA Champions League: 2021 (Chelsea) ⚽ FIFA World Club Cup: 2021 (Chelsea), 2022 ⚽ UEFA Europa League 2019 (Chelsea) ⚽ UEFA Super Cup: 2021 (Chelsea), 2022 ⚽ FA Cup: 2018 ⚽ Copa del Rey: 2023

INTERNATIONAL HONOURS
- FIFA Confederations Cup: 2017

ACTIVITY AREAS

STEFAN SAVIĆ

Stefan Savić reads the game well but his biggest strength is his ability in the air. He is comfortable on the ball and neat with his short passing, relying on brains rather than brawn to operate effectively at the back.

NATIONALITY Montenegran

CURRENT CLUB Atlético Madrid

15

BIRTHDATE	08/01/1991
POSITION	CENTRAL
HEIGHT	1.87 M
WEIGHT	81 KG
PREFERRED FOOT	RIGHT

- APPEARANCES: 356
- BLOCKS: 205
- INTERCEPTIONS: 628
- PENALTIES SCORED: 0
- AERIAL DUELS WON: 64%
- PASS COMPLETION: 85%
- GOALS: 8
- KEY PASSES: 45
- CLEARANCES: 1716
- TACKLES: 472

MAJOR CLUB HONOURS
- La Liga: 2021
- UEFA Europa League: 2018
- UEFA Super Cup: 2018
- Premier League: 2012 (Man City)

INTERNATIONAL HONOURS
- None to date

ACTIVITY AREAS

6

| NATIONALITY | Brazilian |
| CURRENT CLUB | Chelsea |

THIAGO SILVA

Players past and present rate Thiago Silva as one of the best-ever central defenders to play the game. In addition to his technical strengths, he is a natural leader who is able to inspire team-mates to raise their game in the heat of battle.

BIRTHDATE	22/09/1984
POSITION	CENTRAL
HEIGHT	1.83 M
WEIGHT	79 KG
PREFERRED FOOT	RIGHT

- APPEARANCES 484
- BLOCKS 334
- INTERCEPTIONS 1018
- AERIAL DUELS WON 72%
- PASS COMPLETION 93%
- PENALTIES SCORED 0
- GOALS 23
- KEY PASSES 107
- TACKLES 714
- CLEARANCES 2440

MAJOR CLUB HONOURS
- UEFA Champions League: 2021, runner-up 2020 (PSG)
- UEFA Super Cup: 2021 • FIFA Club World Cup: 2021
- Serie A: 2011 (AC Milan) • Ligue 1: 2013-2020 (PSG)
- Coupe de France: 2015-18, 2020 (all PSG) • FA Cup: 2022

INTERNATIONAL HONOURS
- FIFA Confederations Cup: 2013
- Copa América: 2019, runner-up 2021

ACTIVITY AREAS

MILAN ŠKRINIAR

Centre-back Milan Škriniar is a forceful tackler, strong in the air and combative on the ground. But what sets Škriniar apart are his ball-playing skills, ability to stay calm under pressure and pick out intelligent passes.

NATIONALITY
Slovakian

CURRENT CLUB
Inter Milan

37

BIRTHDATE	11/02/1995
POSITION	CENTRAL
HEIGHT	1.87 M
WEIGHT	80 KG
PREFERRED FOOT	RIGHT

APPEARANCES 266
BLOCKS 181
INTERCEPTIONS 246
PENALTIES SCORED 0
AERIAL DUELS WON 52%
PASS COMPLETION 92%
GOALS 11
KEY PASSES 62
CLEARANCES 885
TACKLES 430

MAJOR CLUB HONOURS
⚽ Serie A: 2021 ⚽ UEFA Champions League: runner-up 2023 ⚽ UEFA Europa League: runner-up 2020 ⚽ Coppa Italia: 2022, 2023

INTERNATIONAL HONOURS
⚽ King's Cup: 2018

ACTIVITY AREAS

29

NATIONALITY	French
CURRENT CLUB	Bayern Munich

DAYOT UPAMECANO

Dayot Upamecano has developed into an exceptional centre-half with all the talents needed for the position. His standout talent is his ability with the ball at his feet — a quality that complements his passing accuracy.

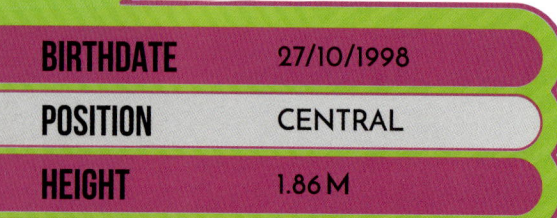

BIRTHDATE	27/10/1998
POSITION	CENTRAL
HEIGHT	1.86 M
WEIGHT	83 KG
PREFERRED FOOT	RIGHT

- APPEARANCES: 221
- INTERCEPTIONS: 341
- AERIAL DUELS WON: 61%
- PASS COMPLETION: 88%
- GOALS: 5
- TACKLES: 449
- CLEARANCES: 677
- KEY PASSES: 58
- PENALTIES SCORED: 0
- BLOCKS: 82

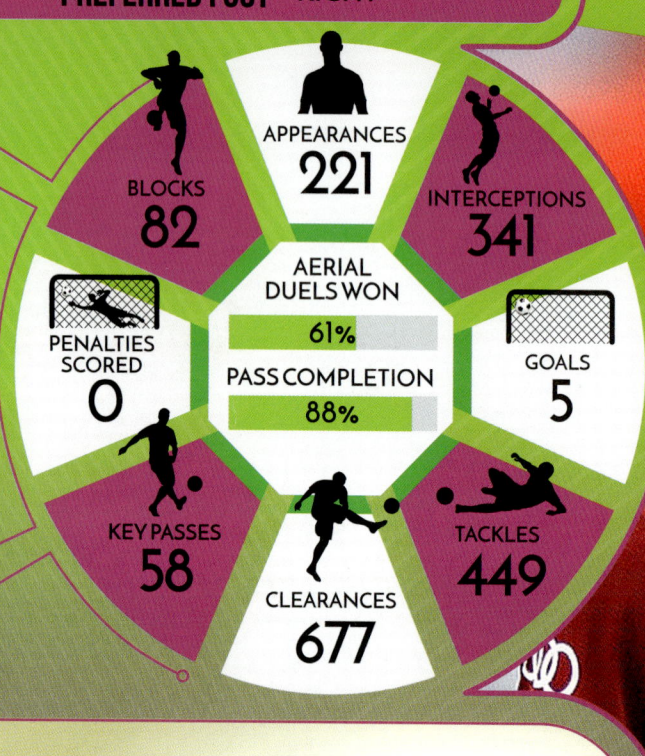

MAJOR CLUB HONOURS
- Bundesliga: 2022, 2023
- DFL Supercup: 2021

INTERNATIONAL HONOURS
- UEFA Nations League: 2021
- FIFA World Cup: runner-up 2022

ACTIVITY AREAS

RAPHAËL VARANE

While most defenders peak in their late 20s, Raphaël Varane was already a star in his teens. Accurate with both feet, an excellent tackler and great in the air, Varane can also launch attacks with his sharp passing and even score goals.

NATIONALITY French

CURRENT CLUB Manchester United

19

BIRTHDATE	25/04/1993
POSITION	CENTRAL
HEIGHT	1.91 M
WEIGHT	81 KG
PREFERRED FOOT	RIGHT

APPEARANCES 398
INTERCEPTIONS 546
GOALS 13
TACKLES 460
CLEARANCES 1719
KEY PASSES 67
PENALTIES SCORED 0
BLOCKS 201
AERIAL DUELS WON 70%
PASS COMPLETION 88%

MAJOR CLUB HONOURS
⚽ La Liga: 2012, 2017, 2020 (R. Madrid) ⚽ UEFA Champions League: 2014, 2016, 2017, 2018 (R. Madrid) ⚽ UEFA Super Cup: 2014, 2016, 2017 (R. Madrid) ⚽ FIFA Club World Cup: 2014, 2016, 2017, 2018 (R. Madrid) ⚽ FA Cup: runner-up 2023

INTERNATIONAL HONOURS
⚽ FIFA World Cup: 2018, runner-up 2022
⚽ UEFA Nations League: 2021

ACTIVITY AREAS

MIDFIELDERS

Midfielders are the heartbeat of a team. Not only do they play between the forwards and the defenders but they also help out their team-mates at both ends. Midfielders fall into one of four main categories: 1) defensive midfielders, who sit in front of the back four and are great tacklers; 2) the attacking full-backs operating on the wings, who whip crosses into the box; 3) the central midfielders, who are brilliant at setting up and then joining attacks, as well as helping out in defence whenever needed; 4) the playmakers — these are the stars who build the attack with their creative play.

WHAT DO THE STATS MEAN?

ASSISTS
A pass, cross or header to a team-mate who then scores counts as an assist. This stat also includes a deflected shot that is converted by a team-mate.

SHOTS
Any deliberate strike on goal counts as a shot. The strike does not have to be on target or force a save from the keeper.

CHANCES CREATED
Any pass that results in a shot at goal (whether or not the goal is scored) is regarded as a chance created.

TACKLES
This is the number of times the player has challenged and dispossessed the opposition without committing a foul.

DRIBBLES
This is the number of times the player has gone past an opponent while running with the ball.

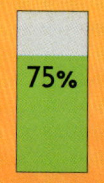

SUCCESSFUL PASSES
This shows as a percentage how successful the midfielder is at finding team-mates with passes, whether over five or 60 yards.

Did you know?

In top-level football, midfielders tend to cover the most ground during the course of a match. A midfielder playing the full 90 minutes will usually run anywhere between 9.5 and 12km.

JUDE BELLINGHAM

NATIONALITY
English

CURRENT CLUB
Real Madrid

5

Jude Bellingham's talent was evident in 2019 when he was just 16 years old! Now he has fulfilled that promise and become one of the world's best midfielders. He is a good tackler, exceptionally quick, positionally aware, and his vision allows him to create and score goals.

BIRTHDATE	29/06/2003
POSITION	CENTRAL
HEIGHT	1.86 M
WEIGHT	75 KG
PREFERRED FOOT	RIGHT

- APPEARANCES: 117
- ASSISTS: 21
- DRIBBLES: 367
- PASSES: 5179
- SUCCESSFUL PASSES: 84%
- PENALTIES SCORED: 1
- GOALS: 20
- SHOTS: 185
- CHANCES CREATED: 112
- TACKLES: 234

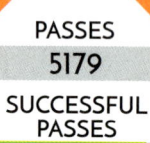

MAJOR CLUB HONOURS
- Bundesliga: runner-up 2023 (Borussia Dortmund)
- DFB-Pokal: 2021 (Borussia Dortmund)

INTERNATIONAL HONOURS
- UEFA European Championship: runner-up 2021

ACTIVITY AREAS

KEVIN DE BRUYNE

Kevin De Bruyne ranks as one of the finest attacking midfielders in the game today. Strong and technically brilliant, he can break up play at one end and almost immediately blast a 25-metre shot into the opposite goal.

NATIONALITY Belgian

CURRENT CLUB Manchester City

17

BIRTHDATE	28/06/1991
POSITION	ATTACKING
HEIGHT	1.81 M
WEIGHT	68 KG
PREFERRED FOOT	RIGHT

- APPEARANCES 408
- ASSISTS 166
- DRIBBLES 1209
- PENALTIES SCORED 5
- PASSES 19677
- SUCCESSFUL PASSES 80%
- GOALS 106
- SHOTS 978
- CHANCES CREATED 1183
- TACKLES 490

MAJOR CLUB HONOURS
- Premier League: 2018, 2019, 2021, 2022, 2023
- UEFA Champions League: runner-up 2021, 2023
- FA Cup: 2019, 2023

INTERNATIONAL HONOURS
- FIFA World Cup: third place 2018

ACTIVITY AREAS

35

5*
*At Barcelona

NATIONALITY
Spanish

CURRENT CLUB
TBC

SERGIO BUSQUETS

Sergio Busquets plays as a deep midfielder who dictates the team's build-up play with clever, short and longer passes. He is great at stopping attacks before they become dangerous and then making passes to launch his team's raids.

BIRTHDATE	16/07/1988
POSITION	DEFENSIVE
HEIGHT	1.89 M
WEIGHT	76 KG
PREFERRED FOOT	RIGHT

ASSISTS 40
APPEARANCES 617
DRIBBLES 426
PENALTIES SCORED 0
PASSES 44100
SUCCESSFUL PASSES 91%
GOALS 16
SHOTS 152
CHANCES CREATED 389
TACKLES 1576

MAJOR CLUB HONOURS
⚽ La Liga: 2009-11, 2013, 2015 2016, 2018, 2019, 2023 (All Barca) ⚽ UEFA Champions League: 2009, 2011, 2015 (all Barca) ⚽ UEFA Super Cup: 2009, 2011, 2015 (all Barca) ⚽ FIFA Club World Cup: 2009, 2011, 2015 (all barca)

INTERNATIONAL HONOURS
⚽ FIFA World Cup: 2010 ⚽ UEFA European Championship: 2012 ⚽ FIFA Confederations Cup: runner-up 2013 ⚽ UEFA Nations League: runner-up 2021

ACTIVITY AREAS

EMRE CAN

Having been a defender earlier in his career, Emre Can has grown into a classy central midfielder. He combines his excellent tackling strength with his midfielder's instincts to thread passes to team-mates in attacking positions.

NATIONALITY
German

CURRENT CLUB
Borussia Dortmund

23

BIRTHDATE	12/01/1994
POSITION	CENTRAL
HEIGHT	1.86 M
WEIGHT	86 KG
PREFERRED FOOT	RIGHT

- ASSISTS: 18
- APPEARANCES: 333
- DRIBBLES: 584
- PENALTIES SCORED: 6
- PASSES: 16389
- SUCCESSFUL PASSES: 85%
- GOALS: 30
- SHOTS: 305
- CHANCES CREATED: 211
- TACKLES: 720

MAJOR CLUB HONOURS

⚽ Bundesliga: 2013 (B. Mun.), runner-up 2023 ⚽ UEFA Champions League: 2013 (B. Mun.), runner-up 2018 (Liverpool) ⚽ UEFA Europa League: runner-up 2016 (Liverpool) ⚽ Serie A: 2019, 2020 (Juventus) ⚽ DFB-Pokal: 2013 (B. Mun), 2021

INTERNATIONAL HONOURS

⚽ FIFA Confederations Cup: 2017

ACTIVITY AREAS

18

NATIONALITY Brazilian

CURRENT CLUB Manchester United

CASEMIRO

Casemiro's strengths are great energy, a high work rate and good support play. Strong, mobile and hard-tackling, his best position is as a defensive midfielder, though his mobility helps him get from box to box and he can also play at centre-back.

BIRTHDATE	23/02/1992
POSITION	CENTRAL
HEIGHT	1.85 M
WEIGHT	84 KG
PREFERRED FOOT	RIGHT

- APPEARANCES 343
- ASSISTS 26
- DRIBBLES 253
- PENALTIES SCORED 0
- PASSES 18255
- SUCCESSFUL PASSES 85%
- GOALS 35
- SHOTS 385
- CHANCES CREATED 219
- TACKLES 1038

MAJOR CLUB HONOURS

⚽ La Liga: 2017, 2020, 2022 (all R. Mad) ⚽ UEFA Champs League: 2014, 2016, 2017, 2018, 2022 (all R. Mad) ⚽ UEFA Super Cup: 2016, 2017, 2022 (all R. Mad) ⚽ FIFA Club World Cup: 2016, 2017, 2018 (all R. Mad) ⚽ FA Cup: runner-up 2023

INTERNATIONAL HONOURS

⚽ FIFA U-20 World Cup: 2011
⚽ Copa América: 2019, runner-up 2021

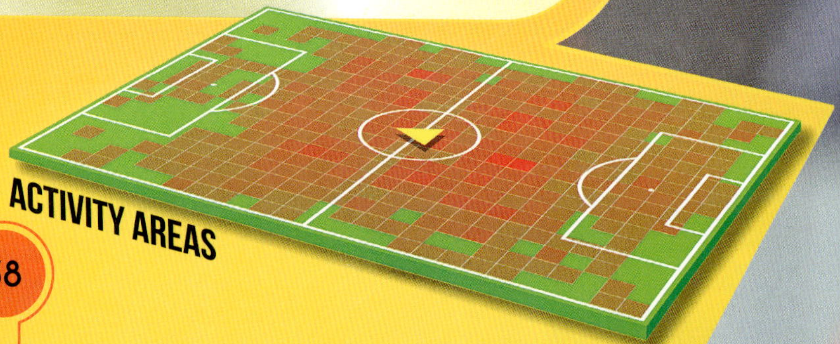

ACTIVITY AREAS

38

PHILIPPE COUTINHO

Philippe Coutinho brings Brazilian flair to the proceedings whenever he steps on to the pitch. Highly skilled with both feet, he is the type of attacking midfielder opposition defenders hate to face in one-on-one situations.

NATIONALITY Brazilian
CURRENT CLUB Aston Villa

23

BIRTHDATE	12/06/1992
POSITION	ATTACKING
HEIGHT	1.72 M
WEIGHT	68 KG
PREFERRED FOOT	RIGHT

- ASSISTS: 67
- APPEARANCES: 401
- DRIBBLES: 1399
- PENALTIES SCORED: 3
- PASSES: 14812
- SUCCESSFUL PASSES: 82%
- GOALS: 95
- SHOTS: 1038
- CHANCES CREATED: 578
- TACKLES: 453

MAJOR CLUB HONOURS
⚽ Bundesliga: 2020 (Bayern Munich) ⚽ La Liga: 2018, 2019 (Barcelona) ⚽ UEFA Champions League: 2020 (B. Munich) ⚽ DFB-Pokal: 2020 (Bayern Munich) ⚽ Copa del Rey: 2018, 2021 (Barcelona) ⚽ Copa Italia: 2011 (Inter Milan)

INTERNATIONAL HONOURS
⚽ Copa América: 2019
⚽ FIFA U-20 World Cup: 2011

ACTIVITY AREAS

39

3

NATIONALITY
Brazilian

CURRENT CLUB
Liverpool

FABINHO

A hard worker in front of defence, Fabinho is a fan favourite at Liverpool. Tall and strong, he is a master at keeping possession for his team and starting the attack from deep. His heat map shows how dominant he is in midfield.

BIRTHDATE	23/10/1993
POSITION	DEFENSIVE
HEIGHT	1.88 M
WEIGHT	78 KG
PREFERRED FOOT	RIGHT

APPEARANCES 396
ASSISTS 21
DRIBBLES 426
PENALTIES SCORED 19
PASSES 20282
SUCCESSFUL PASSES 86%
GOALS 34
SHOTS 221
CHANCES CREATED 240
TACKLES 992

MAJOR CLUB HONOURS
- Premier League: 2020
- UEFA Champions League: 2019
- UEFA Super Cup: 2019
- FIFA Club World Cup: 2019
- Ligue 1: 2017 (Monaco)
- FA Cup: 2022

INTERNATIONAL HONOURS
- Copa América: 2019, runner-up 2021

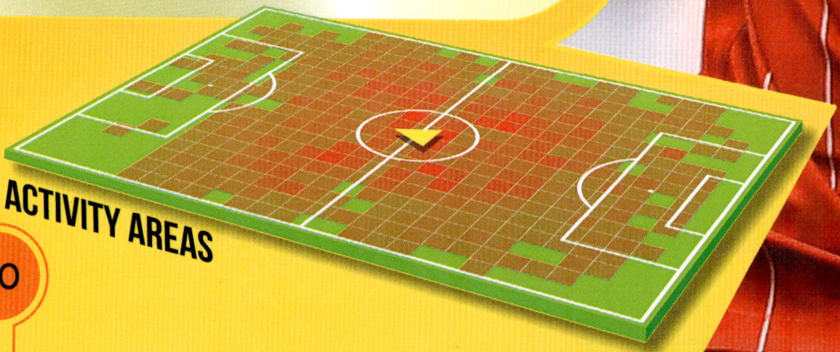

ACTIVITY AREAS

40

BRUNO FERNANDES

Bruno Fernandes shines as a central or attacking midfielder. A sound defensive player, he has a fantastic eye for creating chances with through balls, driving powerful shots from long range and is superb with penalties and free-kicks.

NATIONALITY Portuguese
CURRENT CLUB Manchester United

BIRTHDATE	08/09/1994
POSITION	ATTACKING
HEIGHT	1.79 M
WEIGHT	69 KG
PREFERRED FOOT	RIGHT

APPEARANCES 306
ASSISTS 69
DRIBBLES 540
PENALTIES SCORED 26
PASSES 12974
SUCCESSFUL PASSES 77%
GOALS 84
SHOTS 742
CHANCES CREATED 647
TACKLES 453

MAJOR CLUB HONOURS
⚽ UEFA Europa League: runner-up 2021 ⚽ Taça de Portugal: 2019 (Sporting CP) ⚽ Taça de Liga: 2018, 2019 (Sporting CP) ⚽ FA Cup: runner-up 2023

INTERNATIONAL HONOURS
⚽ UEFA Nations League: 2019

ACTIVITY AREAS

41

ENZO FERNÁNDEZ

NATIONALITY Argentinian
CURRENT CLUB Chelsea

5

BIRTHDATE	17/01/2001
POSITION	CENTRAL
HEIGHT	1.78 M
WEIGHT	76 KG
PREFERRED FOOT	RIGHT

Enzo Fernandez has enjoyed a meteoric rise, highlighted by his award as FIFA Best Young Player at the 2022 World Cup. Playing in central midfield, he is happy to help his defenders, while his exceptionally accurate long-range passing often launches dangerous attacks.

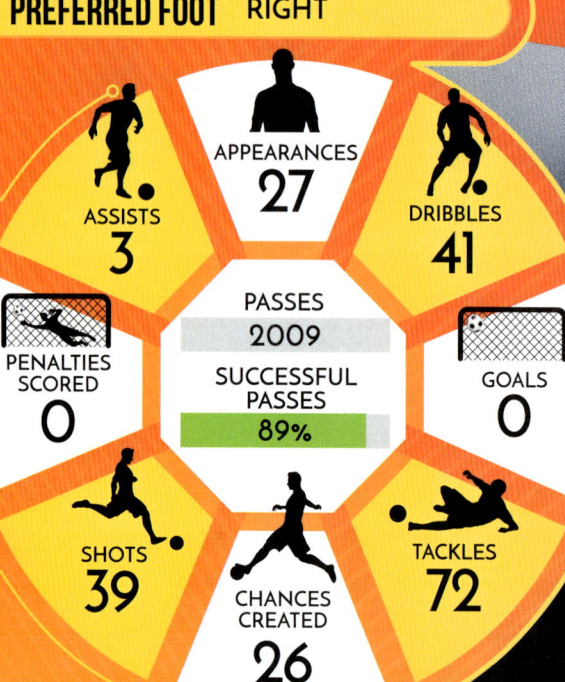

- ASSISTS: 3
- APPEARANCES: 27
- DRIBBLES: 41
- PENALTIES SCORED: 0
- PASSES: 2009
- SUCCESSFUL PASSES: 89%
- GOALS: 0
- SHOTS: 39
- CHANCES CREATED: 26
- TACKLES: 72

MAJOR CLUB HONOURS
- Argentina Primera División: 2021 (River Plate)

INTERNATIONAL HONOURS
- FIFA World Cup: 2022

ACTIVITY AREAS

42

ROBERTO FIRMINO

Roberto Firmino is a box-to-box midfielder with great energy and a perfect passing technique over both long and short distances. He usually plays as a second attacker with a superb left foot, but also surprises defenders with his heading ability.

NATIONALITY Brazilian

CURRENT CLUB TBC

9* *At Liverpool

BIRTHDATE	02/10/1991
POSITION	ATT/STRIKER
HEIGHT	1.81 M
WEIGHT	76 KG
PREFERRED FOOT	RIGHT

- APPEARANCES 466
- ASSISTS 88
- DRIBBLES 1661
- PENALTIES SCORED 5
- PASSES 15496
- SUCCESSFUL PASSES 77%
- GOALS 143
- SHOTS 1033
- CHANCES CREATED 688
- TACKLES 805

MAJOR CLUB HONOURS
⚽ Premier League: 2020 (Liv'pool) ⚽ UEFA Champ. League: 2019, runner-up 2022 (all Liv'pool) ⚽ UEFA Europa League: runner-up 2016 (Liv'pool) ⚽ UEFA Super Cup: 2019 (Liv'pool) ⚽ FIFA Club World Cup: 2019 (Liv'pool) ⚽ FA Cup: 2022 (Liv'pool)

INTERNATIONAL HONOURS
⚽ Copa América: 2019, runner-up 2021

ACTIVITY AREAS

43

10

NATIONALITY
English

CURRENT CLUB
Manchester City

JACK GREALISH

Jack Grealish is among the finest attacking midfielders in Europe. He displays tight ball control, dribbling ability, change of speed and can shoot or deliver dangerous balls into the penalty area from the right or central positions.

BIRTHDATE	10/05/1995
POSITION	ATTACKING
HEIGHT	1.75 M
WEIGHT	76 KG
PREFERRED FOOT	RIGHT

ASSISTS 29
APPEARANCES 170
DRIBBLES 538
PENALTIES SCORED 0
PASSES 5676
SUCCESSFUL PASSES 86%
GOALS 24
SHOTS 264
CHANCES CREATED 353
TACKLES 136

MAJOR CLUB HONOURS
⚽ Premier League: 2022, 2023 ⚽ UEFA Champions League: 2023 ⚽ FA Cup: runner-up 2015 (Aston Villa), 2023

INTERNATIONAL HONOURS
⚽ UEFA European Championship: runner-up 2020

ACTIVITY AREAS

44

FRENKIE DE JONG

Frenkie de Jong has been an outstanding talent ever since he burst on to the scene as a teenager. His close control, accuracy, work rate, passing accuracy and movement have seen him being compared to the great Johan Cruyff.

NATIONALITY Dutch
CURRENT CLUB Barcelona

21

BIRTHDATE	12/05/1997
POSITION	CENTRAL
HEIGHT	1.80 M
WEIGHT	74 KG
PREFERRED FOOT	RIGHT

ASSISTS 16
APPEARANCES 180
DRIBBLES 332
PENALTIES SCORED 0
PASSES 11115
SUCCESSFUL PASSES 91%
GOALS 11
SHOTS 73
CHANCES CREATED 197
TACKLES 229

MAJOR CLUB HONOURS
- La Liga: 2023
- UEFA Europa League: runner-up 2017 (Ajax)
- Copa del Rey: 2021
- Eredivisie: 2019 (Ajax)
- KNVB Cup: 2019 (Ajax)

INTERNATIONAL HONOURS
- UEFA Nations League: runner-up: 2019

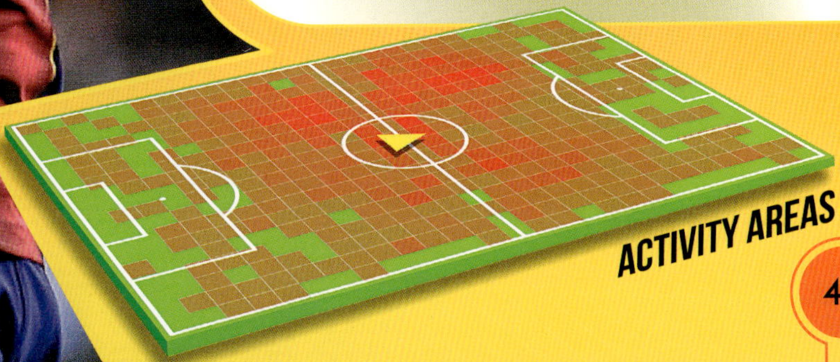

ACTIVITY AREAS

20

NATIONALITY	Italian
CURRENT CLUB	Arsenal

JORGINHO

The talented Jorginho can control the tempo of play from deep, link defence with midfield and midfield with attack with his accurate passing. He has the awareness, vision and passing ability to break lines, and can deliver lofted balls to attacking team-mates.

BIRTHDATE	20/12/1991
POSITION	DEFENSIVE
HEIGHT	1.80 M
WEIGHT	65 KG
PREFERRED FOOT	BOTH

- APPEARANCES 369
- ASSISTS 26
- DRIBBLES 286
- PASSES 27193
- SUCCESSFUL PASSES 89%
- PENALTIES SCORED 32
- GOALS 37
- SHOTS 167
- CHANCES CREATED 379
- TACKLES 759

MAJOR CLUB HONOURS

- Prem. L.: runner-up 2023 ⚽ UEFA Champs. L: 2021 (Chelsea)
- UEFA Europa L: 2019 (Chelsea) ⚽ FIFA World Club Cup: 2021 (Chelsea) ⚽ UEFA Super Cup: 2021 (Chelsea) ⚽ FA Cup: runner-up 2020-22 (Chelsea) ⚽ Coppa Italia: 2014 (Napoli)

INTERNATIONAL HONOURS

- UEFA European Championship: 2020
- UEFA Nations League: third place 2021, third place 2023

ACTIVITY AREAS

46

N'GOLO KANTÉ

Defensive midfielder N'Golo Kanté has pace to burn, boundless energy and great positional awareness. He frequently breaks up attacks with timely tackles, blocks and interceptions, then makes accurate passes. He has a decent eye for goal too.

NATIONALITY French

CURRENT CLUB Chelsea

BIRTHDATE	29/03/1991
POSITION	CENTRAL
HEIGHT	1.68 M
WEIGHT	68 KG
PREFERRED FOOT	RIGHT

APPEARANCES 305
ASSISTS 24
DRIBBLES 608
PENALTIES SCORED 0
PASSES 15191
SUCCESSFUL PASSES 86%
GOALS 14
SHOTS 207
CHANCES CREATED 303
TACKLES 934

MAJOR CLUB HONOURS
- Premier League: 2016 (Leicester City), 2017
- UEFA Champions League: 2021
- UEFA Europa League: 2019
- FIFA Club World Cup: 2021
- UEFA Super Cup: 2021
- FA Cup: 2018, runner-up 2020-22

INTERNATIONAL HONOURS
- FIFA World Cup: 2018
- UEFA European Championship: runner-up 2016

ACTIVITY AREAS

8

NATIONALITY	German
CURRENT CLUB	Real Madrid

TONI KROOS

A set piece specialist who wins challenges in both boxes and dictates the game, Toni Kroos is an athletic box-to-box midfielder who can can pass long and short with either foot. He possesses great vision, creativity and energy.

BIRTHDATE	04/01/1990
POSITION	CENTRAL
HEIGHT	1.83 M
WEIGHT	76 KG
PREFERRED FOOT	RIGHT

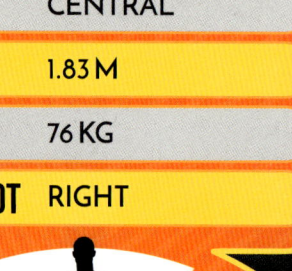

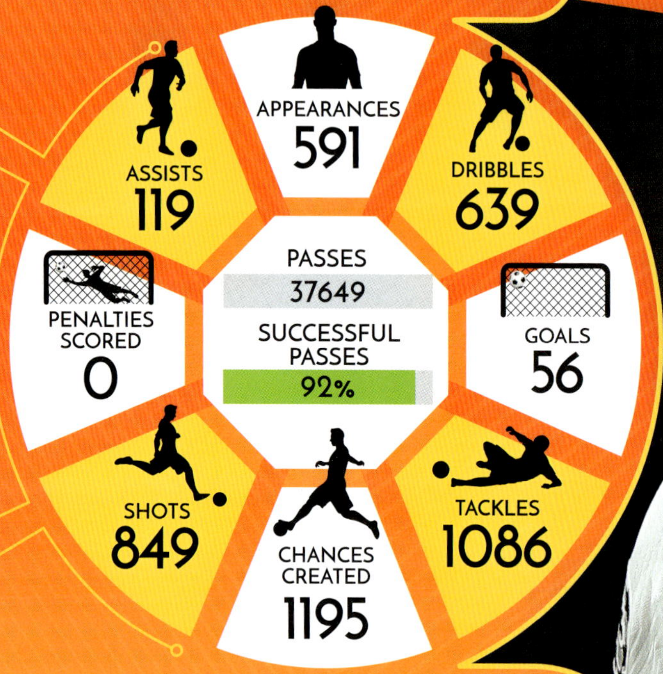

APPEARANCES 591
ASSISTS 119
DRIBBLES 639
PASSES 37649
SUCCESSFUL PASSES 92%
PENALTIES SCORED 0
GOALS 56
SHOTS 849
CHANCES CREATED 1195
TACKLES 1086

MAJOR CLUB HONOURS
⚽ La Liga: 2017, 2020, 2022 ⚽ Bund'liga: 2008, 2013-14 (all B. Mun.) ⚽ UEFA Champs L.: 2013 (B. Mun.), 2016-18, 2022 ⚽ FIFA Club WC: 2013 (B. Mun.), 2014, 2016-18, 2022 ⚽ UEFA Sup. Cup: 2013 (B. Mun), 2014, 2017, 2022 ⚽ Copa del Rey: 2023

INTERNATIONAL HONOURS
⚽ FIFA World Cup: 2014

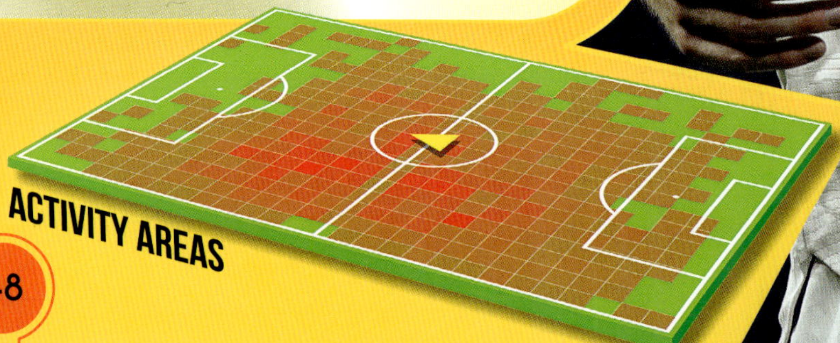

ACTIVITY AREAS

48

SERGEJ MILINKOVIĆ-SAVIĆ

Effective in and around both penalty areas, Sergej Milinković-Savić is a top-class midfielder. He is blessed with great energy and sound technique, and is also good at stopping opposition attacks and launching his own team's raids.

NATIONALITY Serbian

CURRENT CLUB Lazio

21

BIRTHDATE	27/02/1995
POSITION	CENTRAL
HEIGHT	1.91 M
WEIGHT	82 KG
PREFERRED FOOT	RIGHT

- APPEARANCES 312
- ASSISTS 50
- DRIBBLES 663
- PENALTIES SCORED 0
- PASSES 14806
- SUCCESSFUL PASSES 77%
- GOALS 64
- SHOTS 631
- CHANCES CREATED 396
- TACKLES 502

MAJOR CLUB HONOURS
- Serie A: runner-up 2023
- Coppa Italia: 2019

INTERNATIONAL HONOURS
- UEFA European U-19 Championship: 2013
- FIFA U-20 World Cup: 2015

ACTIVITY AREAS

LUKA MODRIĆ

10

NATIONALITY Croatian

CURRENT CLUB Real Madrid

Playmaker Luka Modrić is often at the heart of his team's best attacking moves. He has a great footballing brain, can deliver long and short passes with both feet and strike powerful long-range shots, especially free-kicks.

BIRTHDATE	09/09/1985
POSITION	ATTACKING
HEIGHT	1.72 M
WEIGHT	66 KG
PREFERRED FOOT	RIGHT

- APPEARANCES 585
- ASSISTS 84
- DRIBBLES 1419
- PENALTIES SCORED 6
- PASSES 32544
- SUCCESSFUL PASSES 89%
- GOALS 51
- SHOTS 705
- CHANCES CREATED 896
- TACKLES 767

MAJOR CLUB HONOURS
⚽ La Liga: 2017, 2020, 2022, runner-up 2023 ⚽ UEFA Champions League: 2014, 2016, 2017, 2018, 2022 ⚽ UEFA Super Cup: 2014, 2016, 2017, 2022 ⚽ FIFA Club World Cup: 2014, 2016, 2017, 2018, 2022 ⚽ Copa del Rey: 2023

INTERNATIONAL HONOURS
⚽ FIFA World Cup: runner-up 2018, third place 2022
⚽ UEFA Nations League: runner-up

ACTIVITY AREAS

50

THOMAS MÜLLER

Thomas Müller is a dangerous attacking midfielder, who scores countless goals playing just behind a lone striker. The German powerhouse is mentally strong, tactically clever and great at finding holes in the opposition's defence.

NATIONALITY German

CURRENT CLUB Bayern Munich

25

BIRTHDATE	13/09/1989
POSITION	SECOND STRIKER
HEIGHT	1.85 M
WEIGHT	76 KG
PREFERRED FOOT	RIGHT

- APPEARANCES 584
- ASSISTS 183
- DRIBBLES 1022
- PASSES 19122
- SUCCESSFUL PASSES 77%
- PENALTIES SCORED 22
- GOALS 197
- SHOTS 1153
- CHANCES CREATED 1103
- TACKLES 614

MAJOR CLUB HONOURS
- Bundesliga: (x 12) 2010-2023
- UEFA Champions League: 2013, 2020
- UEFA Super Cup: 2013, 2020
- FIFA Club World Cup: 2013, 2020

INTERNATIONAL HONOURS
- FIFA World Cup: 2014, third place 2010

ACTIVITY AREAS

51

10

| NATIONALITY | American |
| CURRENT CLUB | Chelsea |

CHRISTIAN PULISIC

Although capable of playing in any attacking position, Christian Pulisic's pace, agility and technical ability have made him most effective on the left wing. He also likes to have the ball at his feet, dribbling past opponents to create shooting opportunities for himself.

BIRTHDATE	18/09/1998
POSITION	RIGHT
HEIGHT	1.79 M
WEIGHT	69 KG
PREFERRED FOOT	RIGHT

- ASSISTS: 32
- APPEARANCES: 242
- DRIBBLES: 998
- PENALTIES SCORED: 0
- PASSES: 5161
- SUCCESSFUL PASSES: 80%
- GOALS: 40
- SHOTS: 324
- CHANCES CREATED: 219
- TACKLES: 206

MAJOR CLUB HONOURS
- UEFA Champions League: 2021
- UEFA Super Cup: 2021
- FIFA Club World Cup: 2021
- FA Cup: 2020, 2021, 2022 (all runner-up)
- DFB-Pokal: 2017 (Borussia Dortmund)

INTERNATIONAL HONOURS
- CONCACAF Nations League: 2020
- ONCACAF Gold Cup: 2019: runner-up

ACTIVITY AREAS

52

BUKAYO SAKA

A rising star in world football, Buyako Saka's versatility is just one of his talents. Equally good on both sides at full-back or wing-back, his creativity, positional sense, tackling, shooting and passing talents are displayed best as a right midfielder.

NATIONALITY English
CURRENT CLUB Arsenal

7

BIRTHDATE	05/09/2001
POSITION	WINGER
HEIGHT	1.78 M
WEIGHT	72 KG
PREFERRED FOOT	LEFT

- ASSISTS 34
- APPEARANCES 160
- DRIBBLES 496
- PENALTIES SCORED 4
- PASSES 4595
- SUCCESSFUL PASSES 81%
- GOALS 36
- SHOTS 298
- CHANCES CREATED 237
- TACKLES 186

MAJOR CLUB HONOURS
- Premier League: runner-up 2023
- FA Cup: 2020
- UEFA Europa League: runner-up 2019

INTERNATIONAL HONOURS
- UEFA European Championship: runner-up 2020 (2021)

ACTIVITY AREAS

18

NATIONALITY
Portuguese

CURRENT CLUB
Paris Saint-Germain

RENATO SANCHES

Renato Sanches can play in almost every midfield position: defensive, wide, central or as a creative playmaker. Calm in possession, he is a fine passer, strong tackler and is not afraid of shooting from distance.

BIRTHDATE	18/08/1997
POSITION	CENTRAL
HEIGHT	1.76 M
WEIGHT	70 KG
PREFERRED FOOT	RIGHT

- APPEARANCES 172
- ASSISTS 10
- DRIBBLES 442
- PENALTIES SCORED 0
- PASSES 5930
- SUCCESSFUL PASSES 86%
- GOALS 10
- SHOTS 152
- CHANCES CREATED 133
- TACKLES 125

MAJOR CLUB HONOURS
- Ligue 1: 2021 (Lille), 2023
- Bundesliga: 2017, 2019 (Bayern Munich)
- DFB-Pokal: 2019 (Bayern Munich)
- Premeira Liga: 2016 (Benfica)

INTERNATIONAL HONOURS
- UEFA European Championship: 2016

ACTIVITY AREAS

54

MARCO VERRATTI

Marco Verratti is an awesome ball-playing midfielder. He is able to dribble past defenders at speed to set up chances for the players ahead of him. He can pass or shoot accurately and powerfully with both feet.

NATIONALITY Italian

CURRENT CLUB Paris Saint-Germain

BIRTHDATE	05/11/1992
POSITION	CENTRAL
HEIGHT	1.65 M
WEIGHT	60 KG
PREFERRED FOOT	RIGHT

APPEARANCES 355
ASSISTS 47
DRIBBLES 694
PENALTIES SCORED 0
PASSES 29334
SUCCESSFUL PASSES 91%
GOALS 10
SHOTS 102
CHANCES CREATED 399
TACKLES 981

MAJOR CLUB HONOURS
- Ligue 1: 2013, 2014-16, 2018-20, 2022, 2023
- UEFA Champions League: runner-up 2020
- Coupe de France: 2015, 2016, 2017, 2018, 2020, 2021

INTERNATIONAL HONOURS
- UEFA European Championship: 2020
- UEFA Nations League: third place 2021, third place 2023

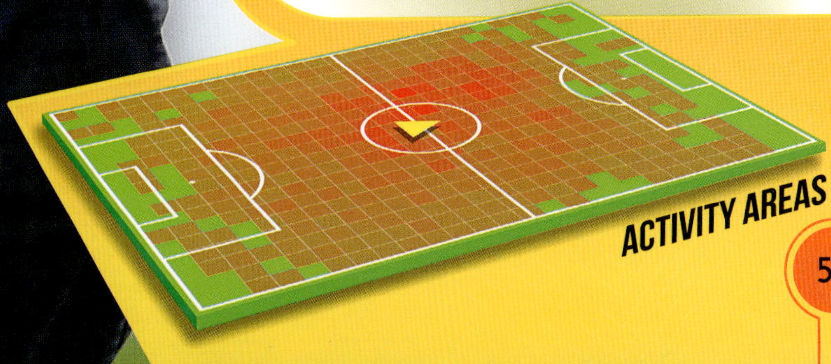

ACTIVITY AREAS

GEORGINIO WIJNALDUM

18

NATIONALITY Dutch

CURRENT CLUB Roma

Georginio Wijnaldum can play anywhere in the middle of the pitch as an attacking playmaker or a defensive shield for the back-line. Good with both feet and a strong tackler, he goes box to box and scores crucial goals, especially with headers.

BIRTHDATE	11/11/1990
POSITION	CENTRAL
HEIGHT	1.75 M
WEIGHT	69 KG
PREFERRED FOOT	RIGHT

- APPEARANCES 344
- ASSISTS 21
- DRIBBLES 596
- PASSES 12836
- SUCCESSFUL PASSES 89%
- PENALTIES SCORED 2
- GOALS 44
- SHOTS 378
- CHANCES CREATED 249
- TACKLES 309

MAJOR CLUB HONOURS
- Ligue 1: 2022 (PSG) Premier League: 2020 (Liv'pool)
- UEFA Champions League: 2019 (Liv'pool), runner-up 2018 (Liv'pool) Europa League: runner-up 2023 UEFA Super Cup: 2019 (Liv'pool) FIFA Club World Cup: 2019 (Liv'pool)

INTERNATIONAL HONOURS
- UEFA Nations League: runner-up: 2019
- FIFA World Cup: third place 2014

ACTIVITY AREAS

56

AXEL WITSEL

Originally a pacy right-winger, Axel Witsel has developed into a strong central midfielder. He frequently drives his team forward with both his play and leadership skills. He is especially good at delivering dangerous passes with either foot.

NATIONALITY Belgian

CURRENT CLUB Atlético Madrid

20

BIRTHDATE	12/01/1989
POSITION	CENTRAL
HEIGHT	1.86 M
WEIGHT	81 KG
PREFERRED FOOT	RIGHT

- APPEARANCES 244
- ASSISTS 11
- DRIBBLES 215
- PENALTIES SCORED 1
- GOALS 20
- SHOTS 200
- CHANCES CREATED 111
- TACKLES 384
- PASSES 13015
- SUCCESSFUL PASSES 92%

MAJOR CLUB HONOURS
- DFL-Pokal: 2021 (Borussia Dortmund)
- DFL-Supercup: 2019 (Borussia Dortmund)

INTERNATIONAL HONOURS
- FIFA World Cup: third place 2018

ACTIVITY AREAS

FORWARDS

The forwards, or strikers, are a team's frontline attackers and the chief goalscorers. They are also the team's most celebrated players. Whether it is the smaller, quicker player, such as Neymar Jr and Mohamed Salah, or the bigger, more physical attacker, such as Erling Haaland and Romelu Lukaku, strikers have perfected the art of finding the back of the net on a regular basis. Aside from scoring lots of goals the world's best strikers are also effective at creating chances for their team-mates.

WHAT DO THE STATS MEAN?

GOALS
This is the total number of goals a striker has scored. The figure spans across all the top clubs the player has represented so far in their career.

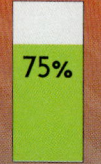

CONVERSION RATE
The percentage shows how good the player is at taking their chance in front of goal. If a player scores two goals from four shots, their conversion rate is 50%.

ASSISTS
A pass, cross or header to a team-mate who then scores counts as an assist. This stat also includes a deflected shot that is immediately converted by a team-mate.

MINUTES PER GOAL
This is the average length of time it takes for the player to score. It is calculated across all the minutes the player has played in their career at top level.

Did you know?

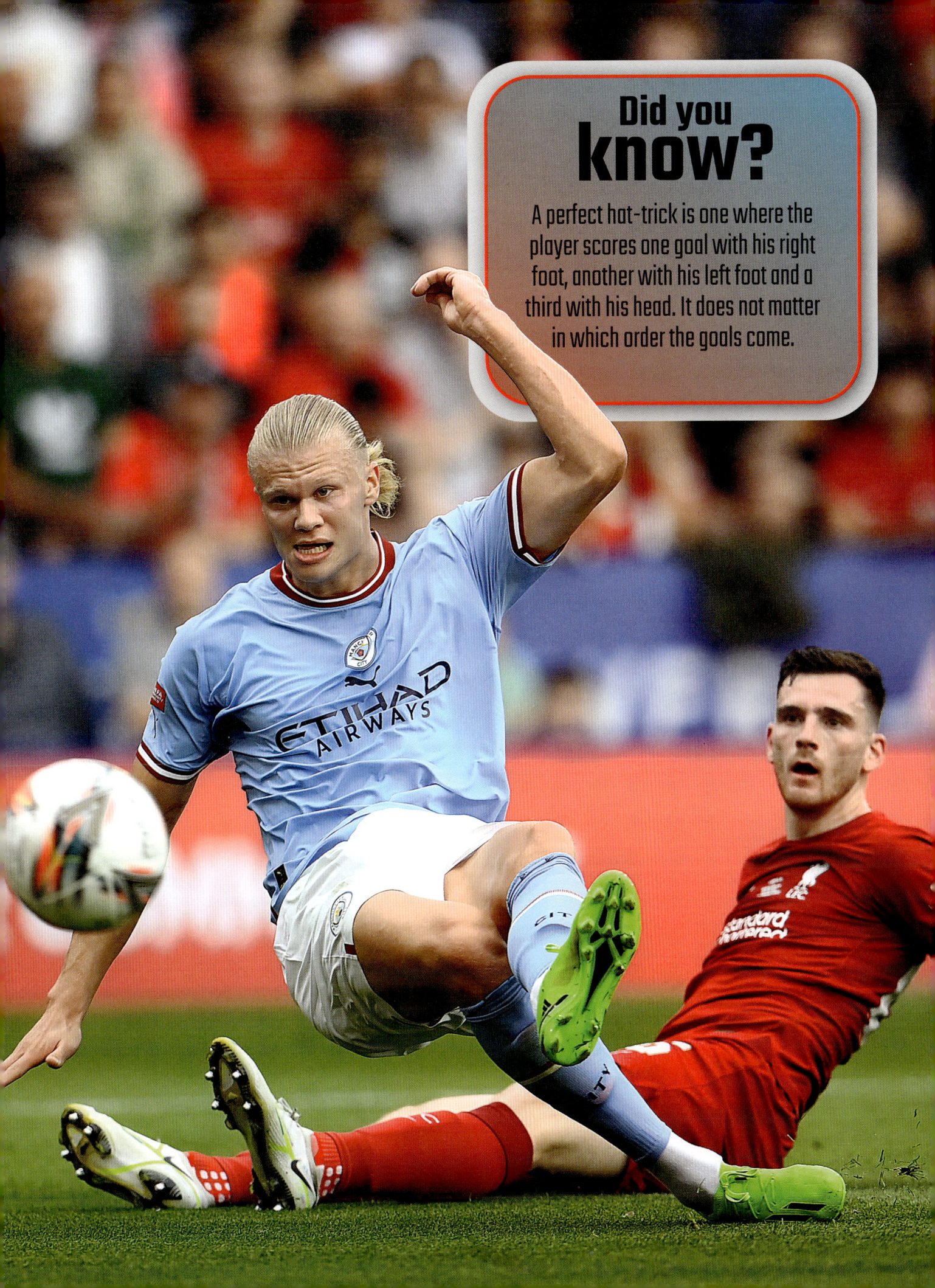

A perfect hat-trick is one where the player scores one goal with his right foot, another with his left foot and a third with his head. It does not matter in which order the goals come.

9*
At Real Madrid

NATIONALITY
French

CURRENT CLUB
TBC

KARIM BENZEMA

Karim Benzema is both a creator and scorer of goals. Intelligent with a great work rate, he can play out wide, down the middle or behind the front man. Although right-footed, he scores many goals with his left and his head.

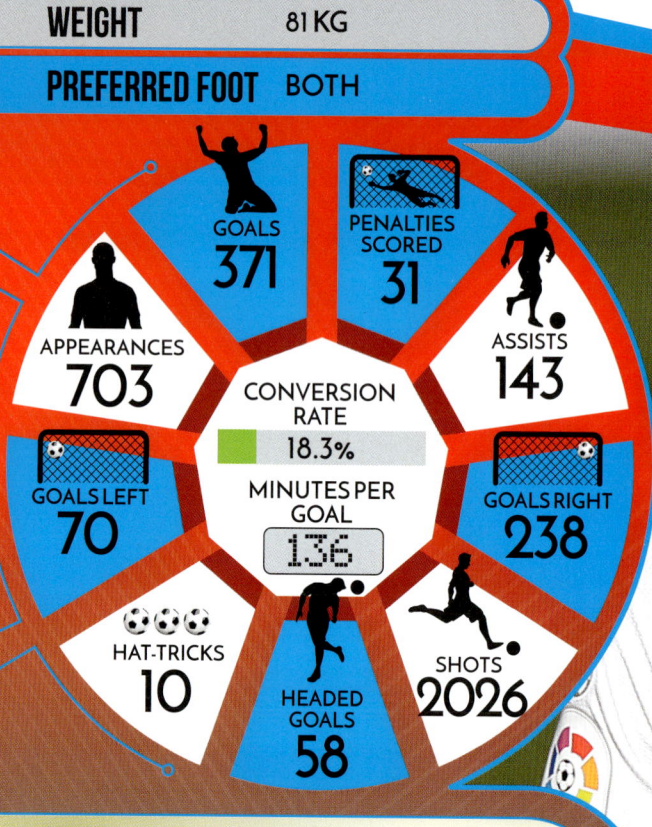

BIRTHDATE	19/12/1987
POSITION	STRIKER
HEIGHT	1.85 M
WEIGHT	81 KG
PREFERRED FOOT	BOTH

- GOALS: 371
- PENALTIES SCORED: 31
- APPEARANCES: 703
- ASSISTS: 143
- CONVERSION RATE: 18.3%
- MINUTES PER GOAL: 136
- GOALS LEFT: 70
- GOALS RIGHT: 238
- HAT-TRICKS: 10
- HEADED GOALS: 58
- SHOTS: 2026

MAJOR CLUB HONOURS
⚽ La Liga: 2012, '17, '20, '22 (R. Mad.) ⚽ UEFA C. League: 2014, 2016-18, '22 (R. Mad) ⚽ FIFA Club WC: 2014, 2016-18, '22 (R. Mad.) ⚽ UEFA S. Cup: 2014, 2016-17, '22 (R. Mad.) ⚽ Ligue 1: 2005-08 (Lyon) ⚽ Copa del Rey: 2023 (R. Mad.)

INTERNATIONAL HONOURS
⚽ UEFA Nations League: 2021
⚽ FIFA World Cup: runner-up 2022

ACTIVITY AREAS

60

EDINSON CAVANI

Edinson Cavani is a fine dribbler, great at running into space and scoring spectacular goals, especially with overhead kicks. He has an impressive work rate too, always hassling the opposition's defence to win the ball.

NATIONALITY
Uruguayan

CURRENT CLUB
TBC

7*
*At Valencia

BIRTHDATE	14/02/1987
POSITION	STRIKER
HEIGHT	1.84 M
WEIGHT	71 KG
PREFERRED FOOT	RIGHT

- GOALS: 320
- PENALTIES SCORED: 47
- ASSISTS: 58
- APPEARANCES: 571
- CONVERSION RATE: 19.7%
- MINUTES PER GOAL: 132
- GOALS LEFT: 50
- GOALS RIGHT: 211
- HAT-TRICKS: 14
- HEADED GOALS: 56
- SHOTS: 1625

MAJOR CLUB HONOURS
- UEFA Champions League: runner-up 2020 (PSG)
- UEFA Europa League: runner-up 2021 (Man Utd)
- Ligue 1: 2014, 2015, 2016, 2018, 2019, 2020 (all PSG)
- Coupe de France: 2015, 2016, 2017, 2018, 2020 (all PSG)

INTERNATIONAL HONOURS
- Copa América: 2011

ACTIVITY AREAS

NATIONALITY Dutch

CURRENT CLUB Atlético Madrid

MEMPHIS DEPAY

Memphis Depay has developed into a world-class striker, though he is still considered to be a left-winger or left-sided striker. He is a brave player and will challenge the biggest defenders in the middle of the danger area.

BIRTHDATE	13/02/1994
POSITION	WINGER
HEIGHT	1.78 M
WEIGHT	78 KG
PREFERRED FOOT	RIGHT

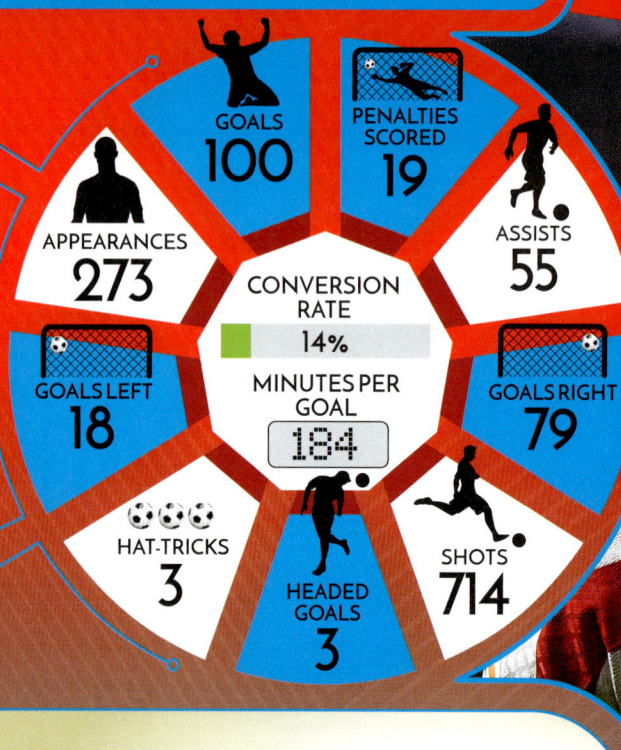

- GOALS: 100
- PENALTIES SCORED: 19
- APPEARANCES: 273
- ASSISTS: 55
- CONVERSION RATE: 14%
- MINUTES PER GOAL: 184
- GOALS LEFT: 18
- GOALS RIGHT: 79
- HAT-TRICKS: 3
- HEADED GOALS: 3
- SHOTS: 714

MAJOR CLUB HONOURS
- Eredivisie: 2015 (PSV Eindhoven)
- KNVB Cup: 2012 (PSV Eindhoven)
- FA Cup: 2016 (Manchester United)

INTERNATIONAL HONOURS
- FIFA World Cup: third place 2014

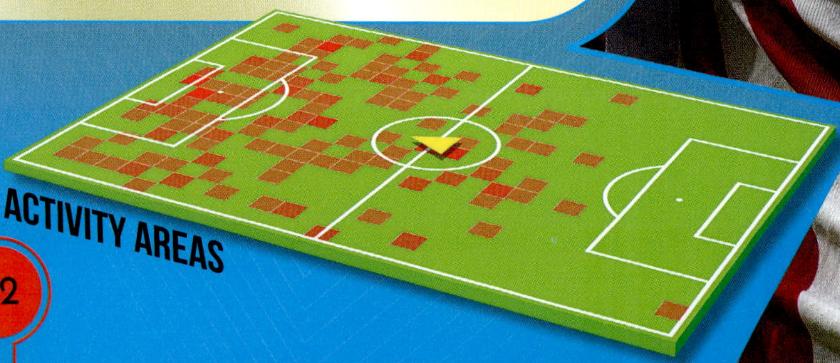

ACTIVITY AREAS

JOÃO FÉLIX

The latest star striker to emerge out of Portugal, João Félix perfected his craft in *La Liga* before making a loan move to the Premier League in 2023. An eye for goal combined with versatility mean he can be deployed as a central striker, second forward, attacking midfielder or winger.

NATIONALITY Portuguese

CURRENT CLUB TBC

11* *At Chelsea

BIRTHDATE	10/11/1999
POSITION	FORWARD
HEIGHT	1.81 M
WEIGHT	70 KG
PREFERRED FOOT	RIGHT

- GOALS: 39
- PENALTIES SCORED: 4
- ASSISTS: 16
- GOALS RIGHT: 28
- SHOTS: 304
- HEADED GOALS: 4
- HAT-TRICKS: 1
- GOALS LEFT: 7
- APPEARANCES: 150
- CONVERSION RATE: 12.8%
- MINUTES PER GOAL: 229

MAJOR CLUB HONOURS
- La Liga: 2021 (Atlético Madrid)
- Primeira Liga: 2019 (Benfica)

INTERNATIONAL HONOURS
- UEFA Nations League: 2019

ACTIVITY AREAS

63

NATIONALITY	French
CURRENT CLUB	AC Milan

OLIVIER GIROUD

Olivier Giroud is much more than a target man because his work-rate and positional sense make him hard to defend against near the goal. He uses his physique to hold and shield the ball, and is known for his accurate passing, shooting and heading.

BIRTHDATE	30/09/1986
POSITION	STRIKER
HEIGHT	1.93 M
WEIGHT	91 KG
PREFERRED FOOT	LEFT

- GOALS: 184
- PENALTIES SCORED: 19
- ASSISTS: 61
- APPEARANCES: 468
- CONVERSION RATE: 15.9%
- MINUTES PER GOAL: 162
- GOALS LEFT: 113
- GOALS RIGHT: 18
- HAT-TRICKS: 7
- HEADED GOALS: 53
- SHOTS: 1154

MAJOR CLUB HONOURS
- Serie A: 2022
- UEFA Champions League: 2021 (Chelsea)
- UEFA Europa League: 2019 (Chelsea)
- Ligue 1: 2012 (Montpellier)
- FA Cup: 2014, 2015, 2017 (Arsenal), 2018 (Chelsea)

INTERNATIONAL HONOURS
- FIFA World Cup 2018, runner-up 2022
- UEFA European Championship: runner-up 2016

ACTIVITY AREAS

64

ANTOINE GRIEZMANN

Known for being the ultimate team player, Antoine Griezmann is able to fulfil all offensive roles, be it front man, attacking midfielder, false 9 or coming from wide positions. He is an excellent team-mate, using his experience to improve everyone around him in all situations.

NATIONALITY
French

CURRENT CLUB
Atlético Madrid

8

BIRTHDATE	21/03/1991
POSITION	STRIKER
HEIGHT	1.76 M
WEIGHT	73 KG
PREFERRED FOOT	LEFT

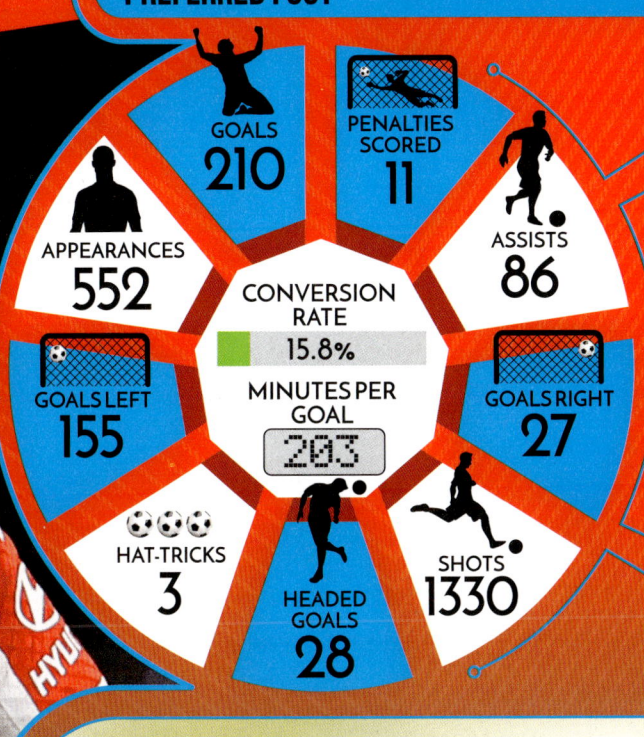

- GOALS: 210
- PENALTIES SCORED: 11
- ASSISTS: 86
- APPEARANCES: 552
- CONVERSION RATE: 15.8%
- MINUTES PER GOAL: 203
- GOALS LEFT: 155
- GOALS RIGHT: 27
- HAT-TRICKS: 3
- HEADED GOALS: 28
- SHOTS: 1330

MAJOR CLUB HONOURS
- UEFA Champions League: runner-up 2016
- UEFA Europa League 2018
- UEFA Super Cup 2018
- Copa del Rey 2021 (Barcelona)

INTERNATIONAL HONOURS
- FIFA World Cup: 2018, runner-up 2022
- UEFA European Championship: runner-up 2016
- UEFA Nations League: 2021

ACTIVITY AREAS

NATIONALITY
Norwegian

CURRENT CLUB
Manchester City

ERLING HAALAND

Erling Haaland has become one of the most exciting forwards in world football. He has all the talents: two good feet, blistering pace, good in the air, energy, strength, timing and the instincts to put the ball in the back of the net.

BIRTHDATE	21/07/2000
POSITION	STRIKER
HEIGHT	1.94 M
WEIGHT	88 KG
PREFERRED FOOT	LEFT

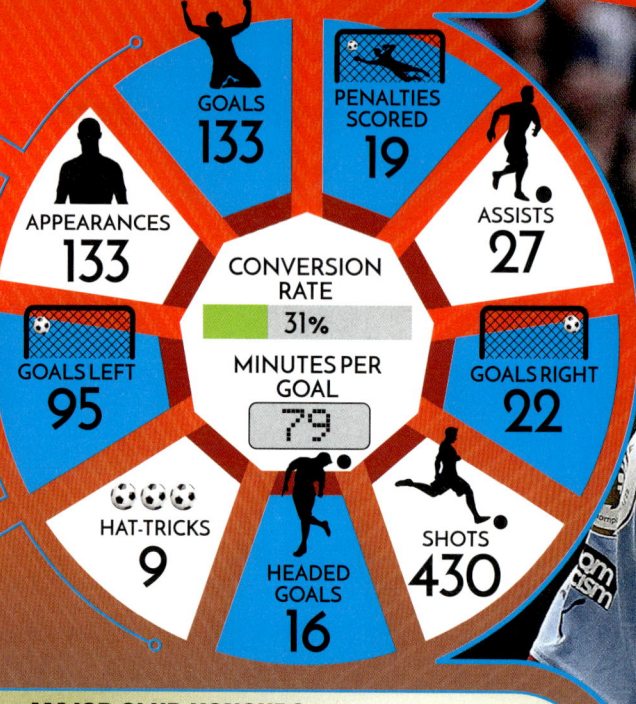

- GOALS: 133
- PENALTIES SCORED: 19
- ASSISTS: 27
- GOALS RIGHT: 22
- SHOTS: 430
- HEADED GOALS: 16
- HAT-TRICKS: 9
- GOALS LEFT: 95
- APPEARANCES: 133
- CONVERSION RATE: 31%
- MINUTES PER GOAL: 79

MAJOR CLUB HONOURS
- Premier League: 2023
- UEFA Champions League: 2023
- DFB-Pokal: 2021 (Borussia Dortmund)
- Austrian Bundesliga: 2019, 2020 (Red Bull Salzburg)
- FA Cup: 2023
- Austrian Cup: 2019 (Red Bull Salzburg)

INTERNATIONAL HONOURS
- None to date

ACTIVITY AREAS

66

CIRO IMMOBILE

A great team-player, Ciro Immobile is a natural finisher who is excellent in the air. His goals tally is even higher because he refuses to give up lost causes and is willing to chase back to force mistakes out of defenders.

NATIONALITY Italian

CURRENT CLUB Lazio

17

BIRTHDATE	20/02/1990
POSITION	STRIKER
HEIGHT	1.85 M
WEIGHT	78 KG
PREFERRED FOOT	RIGHT

- GOALS: 224
- PENALTIES SCORED: 55
- ASSISTS: 56
- APPEARANCES: 398
- CONVERSION RATE: 18.9%
- MINUTES PER GOAL: 132
- GOALS LEFT: 31
- GOALS RIGHT: 169
- HAT-TRICKS: 8
- HEADED GOALS: 24
- SHOTS: 1187

MAJOR CLUB HONOURS
- Serie A: runner-up 2023
- Coppa Italia: 2019

INTERNATIONAL HONOURS
- UEFA European Championship: 2020
- UEFA Nations League: third place 2023

ACTIVITY AREAS

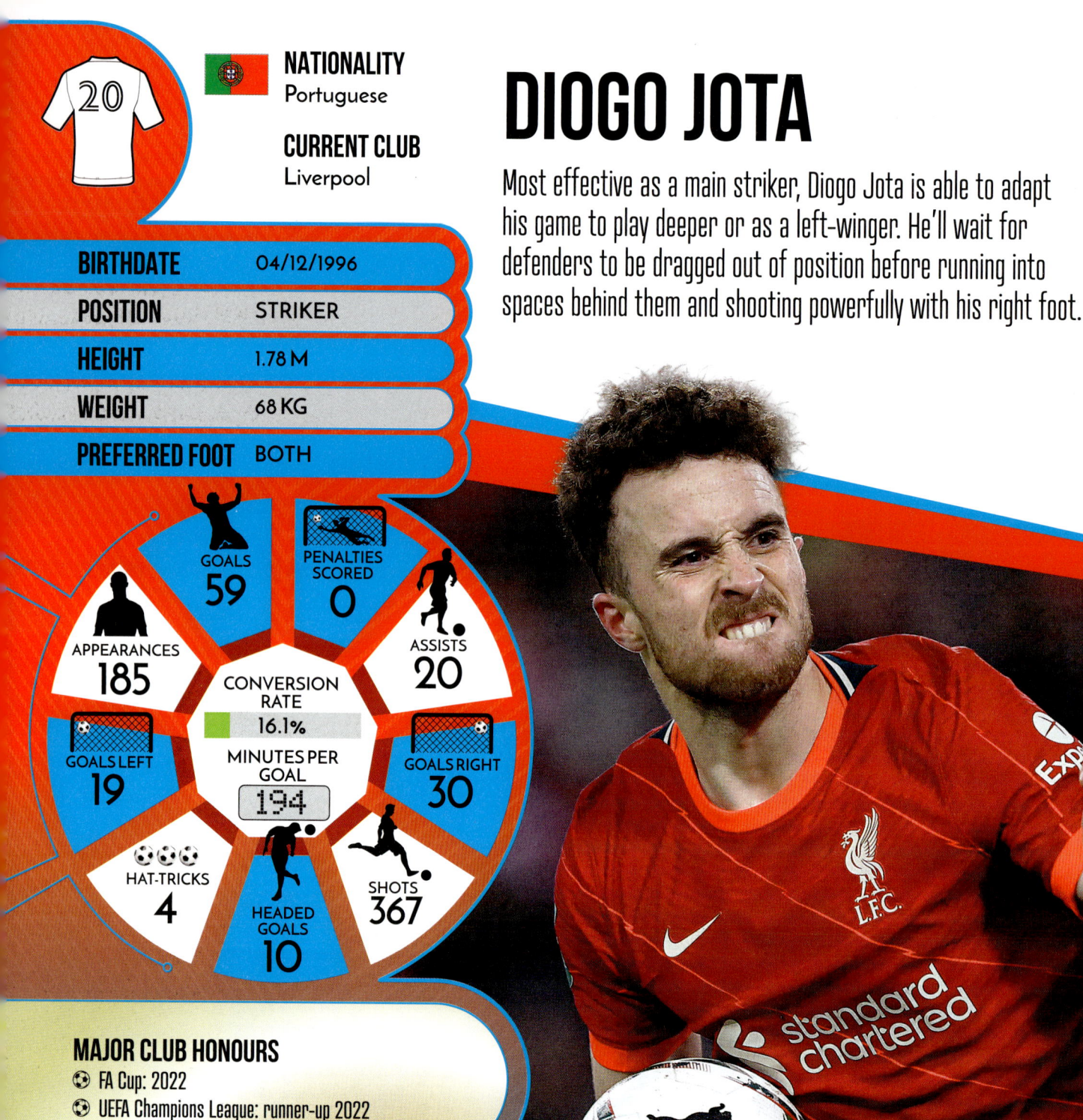

20	

NATIONALITY	Portuguese
CURRENT CLUB	Liverpool

DIOGO JOTA

Most effective as a main striker, Diogo Jota is able to adapt his game to play deeper or as a left-winger. He'll wait for defenders to be dragged out of position before running into spaces behind them and shooting powerfully with his right foot.

BIRTHDATE	04/12/1996
POSITION	STRIKER
HEIGHT	1.78 M
WEIGHT	68 KG
PREFERRED FOOT	BOTH

- GOALS: 59
- PENALTIES SCORED: 0
- ASSISTS: 20
- APPEARANCES: 185
- CONVERSION RATE: 16.1%
- MINUTES PER GOAL: 194
- GOALS LEFT: 19
- GOALS RIGHT: 30
- HAT-TRICKS: 4
- HEADED GOALS: 10
- SHOTS: 367

MAJOR CLUB HONOURS
- FA Cup: 2022
- UEFA Champions League: runner-up 2022

INTERNATIONAL HONOURS
- UEFA Nations League: 2019

ACTIVITY AREAS

LUKA JOVIĆ

Luka Jović is a predator in the penalty box. He uses his speed and attacking instincts to find spaces in the penalty area and score goals from close range with deft touches from either foot and occasionally his head.

NATIONALITY Serbian

CURRENT CLUB Fiorentina

BIRTHDATE	23/12/1997
POSITION	STRIKER
HEIGHT	1.81 M
WEIGHT	78 KG
PREFERRED FOOT	RIGHT

- GOALS: 48
- PENALTIES SCORED: 1
- ASSISTS: 14
- GOALS RIGHT: 24
- SHOTS: 308
- HEADED GOALS: 10
- HAT-TRICKS: 1
- GOALS LEFT: 14
- APPEARANCES: 163
- CONVERSION RATE: 15.6%
- MINUTES PER GOAL: 162

MAJOR CLUB HONOURS
- La Liga: 2020, 2022 (Real Madrid)
- UEFA Champions League: 2022 (Real Madrid)
- DFB-Pokal: 2018 (Eintracht Frankfurt)
- UEFA Conference League: runner-up

INTERNATIONAL HONOURS
- None to date

ACTIVITY AREAS

69

10

NATIONALITY English

CURRENT CLUB Tottenham Hotspur

HARRY KANE

Harry Kane has grown into the complete striker. His power in the air, skills with both feet and superb ball-striking technique make him hard to defend against. What's more, with his defence-splitting passes, he also sets up many goals for his team-mates.

BIRTHDATE	28/07/1993
POSITION	STRIKER
HEIGHT	1.88 M
WEIGHT	86 KG
PREFERRED FOOT	RIGHT

GOALS **245**
PENALTIES SCORED **37**
APPEARANCES **383**
ASSISTS **56**
CONVERSION RATE **17.8%**
MINUTES PER GOAL **128**
GOALS LEFT **47**
GOALS RIGHT **147**
HAT-TRICKS **10**
HEADED GOALS **49**
SHOTS **1373**

MAJOR CLUB HONOURS
- UEFA Champions League: runner-up 2019

INTERNATIONAL HONOURS
- UEFA European Championship: runner-up 2020
- UEFA Nations League: third place 2019

ACTIVITY AREAS

70

ROBERT LEWANDOWSKI

Robert Lewandowski has consistently ranked as one of the world's best strikers since he made his debut at Borussia Dortmund in 2010. His positioning, technique, power and finishing saw him net more than 300 goals in the Bundesliga before he made his move to Barcelona in 2022.

NATIONALITY
Polish

CURRENT CLUB
Barcelona

9

BIRTHDATE	21/08/1988
POSITION	STRIKER
HEIGHT	1.85 M
WEIGHT	81 KG
PREFERRED FOOT	RIGHT

- GOALS: 429
- PENALTIES SCORED: 57
- ASSISTS: 82
- GOALS RIGHT: 284
- SHOTS: 2104
- HEADED GOALS: 68
- HAT-TRICKS: 22
- GOALS LEFT: 73
- APPEARANCES: 545
- CONVERSION RATE: 20.4%
- MINUTES PER GOAL: 103

MAJOR CLUB HONOURS
⚽ La Liga: 2023 ⚽ Bundesliga: 2011, 2012 (all B. Dort.), 2015-22 (x8 all B. Mun.) ⚽ UEFA Champions League: 2020 (B. Mun) ⚽ FIFA Club World Cup: 2020 (B. Mun.) ⚽ UEFA Super Cup: 2020 (B. Mun.)

INTERNATIONAL HONOURS
⚽ None to date

ACTIVITY AREAS

90

NATIONALITY Belgian

CURRENT CLUB Inter Milan (on loan)

ROMELU LUKAKU

Romelu Lukaku often uses his size and strength to dispossess defenders before controlling the ball and unleashing a fierce shot or a pass to a well-placed team-mate. He is also superb in the air and scores many headers.

BIRTHDATE	13/05/1993
POSITION	STRIKER
HEIGHT	1.91 M
WEIGHT	93 KG
PREFERRED FOOT	LEFT

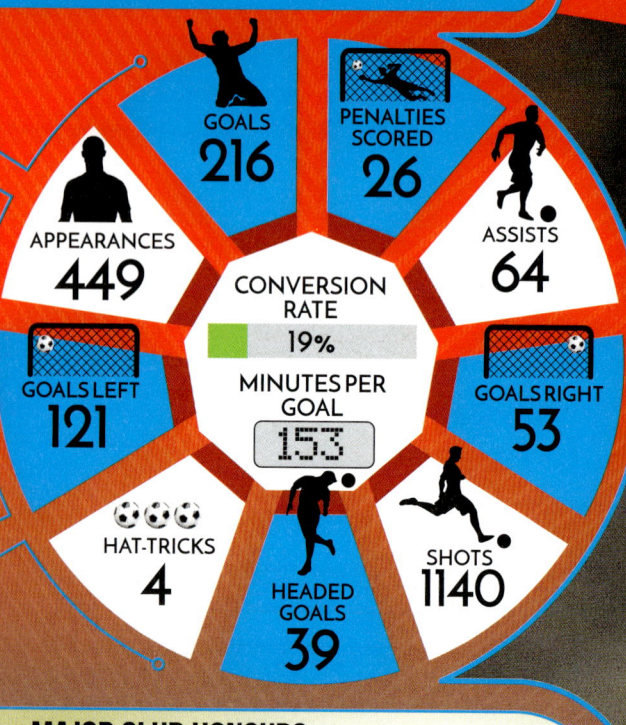

- GOALS: 216
- PENALTIES SCORED: 26
- ASSISTS: 64
- GOALS RIGHT: 53
- SHOTS: 1140
- HEADED GOALS: 39
- HAT-TRICKS: 4
- GOALS LEFT: 121
- APPEARANCES: 449
- CONVERSION RATE: 19%
- MINUTES PER GOAL: 153

MAJOR CLUB HONOURS
⚽ Serie A: 2021 ⚽ UEFA Champions League: runner-up 2023 ⚽ Coppa Italia: 2023 ⚽ FIFA Club World Cup: 2021 (Chelsea) ⚽ UEFA Europa League: runner-up 2020 (Chelsea) ⚽ Belgian Pro League: 2010 (Anderlecht)

INTERNATIONAL HONOURS
⚽ FIFA World Cup: third place 2018

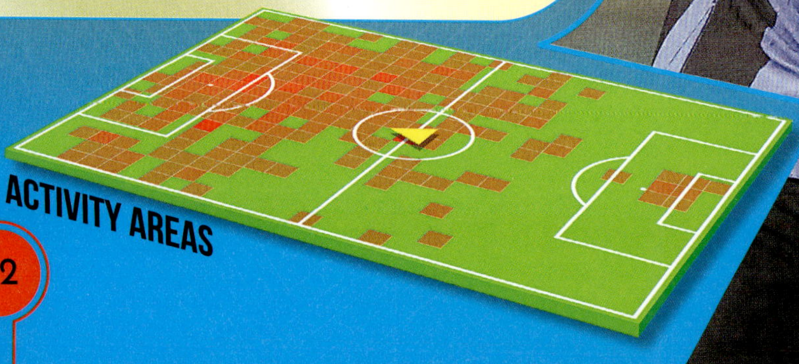

ACTIVITY AREAS

SADIO MANÉ

Sadio Mané has breathtaking pace and dribbling ability. Although he normally plays on the wing, he can also be dangerous in the middle of the park as he can leap high to win headers and shoot powerfully with either foot.

NATIONALITY
Senegalese

CURRENT CLUB
TBC

17*
*At Bayern Munich

BIRTHDATE	10/04/1992
POSITION	WINGER
HEIGHT	1.75 M
WEIGHT	69 KG
PREFERRED FOOT	RIGHT

- GOALS: 149
- PENALTIES SCORED: 1
- ASSISTS: 51
- APPEARANCES: 361
- CONVERSION RATE: 18%
- MINUTES PER GOAL: 185
- GOALS LEFT: 43
- GOALS RIGHT: 86
- HAT-TRICKS: 3
- HEADED GOALS: 20
- SHOTS: 828

MAJOR CLUB HONOURS
⚽ Bundesliga: 2023 ⚽ Prem. League: 2020 (Liv'pool) ⚽ UEFA Champ. League: 2019 (Liv'pool), runner-up 2018 (Liv'pool), runner-up 2022 (Liv'pool) ⚽ UEFA Super Cup: 2019 (Liv'pool) ⚽ FIFA Club World Cup: 2019 (Liv'pool) ⚽ FA Cup: 2022 (Liv'pool)

INTERNATIONAL HONOURS
⚽ CAF Africa Cup of Nations: 2021, runner-up 2019

ACTIVITY AREAS

7

NATIONALITY
French

CURRENT CLUB
Paris Saint-Germain

KYLIAN MBAPPÉ

A FIFA World Cup winner with France at just 18 and a runner-up four years later, Kylian Mbappé is counted among the best strikers in world football today. The pacey finisher is a superb ball-player who consistently gets on the score sheet and sets up chances for his team-mates.

BIRTHDATE	20/12/1998
POSITION	STRIKER
HEIGHT	1.78 M
WEIGHT	75 KG
PREFERRED FOOT	RIGHT

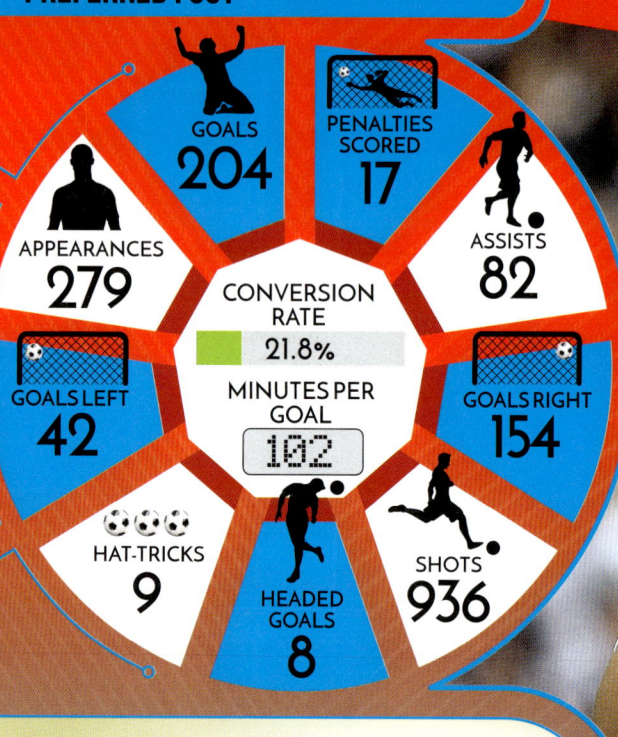

- GOALS: 204
- PENALTIES SCORED: 17
- APPEARANCES: 279
- ASSISTS: 82
- CONVERSION RATE: 21.8%
- MINUTES PER GOAL: 102
- GOALS LEFT: 42
- GOALS RIGHT: 154
- HAT-TRICKS: 9
- HEADED GOALS: 8
- SHOTS: 936

MAJOR CLUB HONOURS
- Ligue 1: 2017 (Monaco), 2018, 2019, 2020, 2022, 2023
- UEFA Champions League: runner-up 2020
- Coupe de France: 2018, 2020, 2021

INTERNATIONAL HONOURS
- FIFA World Cup: 2018, runner-up 2022
- UEFA Nations League: 2021

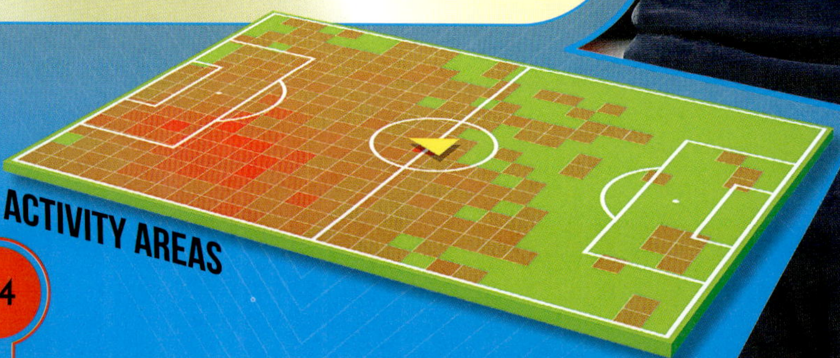

ACTIVITY AREAS

74

LIONEL MESSI

The greatest player of his generation, if not the greatest ever, the 2022 World Cup winner is a fine playmaker with a stunning goal-scoring record. He is also a fantastically fast dribbler who can carve out opportunities to shoot with either foot, from any range.

NATIONALITY
Argentinian

CURRENT CLUB
Inter Miami (MLS)

30*
*At Paris Saint-Germain

BIRTHDATE	24/06/1987
POSITION	FORWARD
HEIGHT	1.70 M
WEIGHT	72 KG
PREFERRED FOOT	LEFT

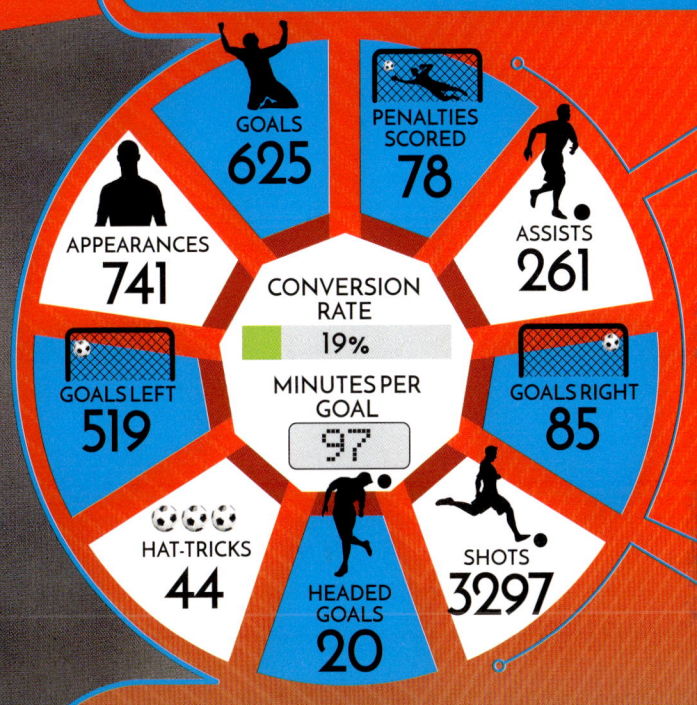

- GOALS: 625
- PENALTIES SCORED: 78
- ASSISTS: 261
- APPEARANCES: 741
- CONVERSION RATE: 19%
- MINUTES PER GOAL: 97
- GOALS LEFT: 519
- GOALS RIGHT: 85
- HAT-TRICKS: 44
- HEADED GOALS: 20
- SHOTS: 3297

MAJOR CLUB HONOURS

⚽ Ligue 1: 2022, 2023 (PSG) ⚽ La Liga: 2005-06, 2009-11, 2013, 2015-16, 2018-19 (all Barca) ⚽ UEFA Champions L.: 2006, 2009, 2011, 2015 (all Barca) ⚽ UEFA Super Cup: 2009, 2011, 2015 (all Barca) ⚽ FIFA Club World Cup: 2009, 2011, 2015 (all Barca)

INTERNATIONAL HONOURS

⚽ FIFA World Cup: 2022, runner-up 2014
⚽ Olympic Games: gold medal 2008
⚽ Copa América: 2021, runner-up 2007, 2015, 2016

ACTIVITY AREAS

75

ÁLVARO MORATA

19

NATIONALITY Spanish

CURRENT CLUB Atlético Madrid

Álvaro Morata is perfectly built for a central striker. Tall, strong and excellent in the air, he is comfortable with the ball at his feet. Morata is also surprisingly fast and has great tactical and positional awareness.

BIRTHDATE	23/10/1992
POSITION	STRIKER
HEIGHT	1.90 M
WEIGHT	84 KG
PREFERRED FOOT	RIGHT

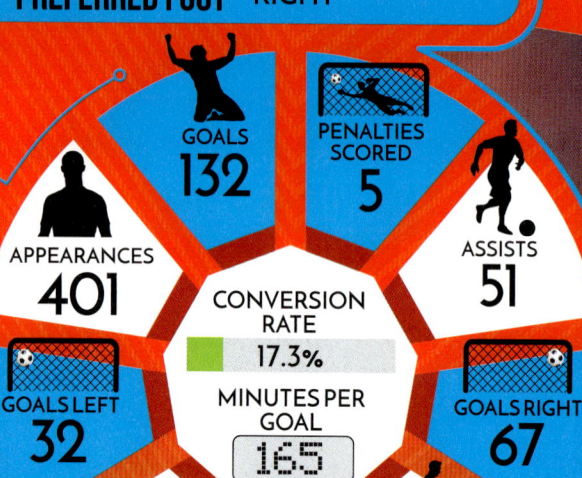

- GOALS: 132
- PENALTIES SCORED: 5
- ASSISTS: 51
- APPEARANCES: 401
- GOALS LEFT: 32
- GOALS RIGHT: 67
- HAT-TRICKS: 2
- HEADED GOALS: 33
- SHOTS: 765
- CONVERSION RATE: 17.3%
- MINUTES PER GOAL: 165

MAJOR CLUB HONOURS
- La Liga: 2012, 2017 (R. Mad.) ⚽ Serie A: 2015, 2016 (Juve.)
- UEFA Champions League: 2014, 2017 (R. Mad.), runner-up 2015 (Juve.) ⚽ UEFA Europa League: 2019 (Chelsea) ⚽ UEFA Super Cup: 2016 (R. Mad.) ⚽ FIFA Club World Cup: 2016 (R. Mad.)

INTERNATIONAL HONOURS
- ⚽ UEFA European U-21 Championship: 2013
- ⚽ UEFA Nations League: 2023

ACTIVITY AREAS

NEYMAR JR

Neymar is the latest in the long line of great Brazilian strikers. His pace and phenomenal dribbling help him beat defenders in numbers. He strikes fear into the opposition defence with his energetic pace and playmaking skills.

NATIONALITY
Brazilian

CURRENT CLUB
Paris Saint-Germain

10

BIRTHDATE	05/02/1992
POSITION	FORWARD
HEIGHT	1.75 M
WEIGHT	68 KG
PREFERRED FOOT	RIGHT

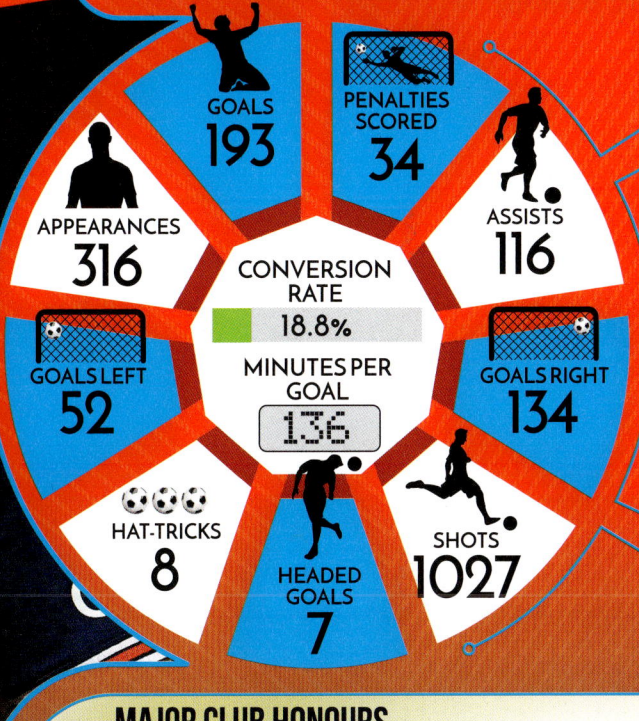

- GOALS: 193
- PENALTIES SCORED: 34
- ASSISTS: 116
- GOALS RIGHT: 134
- SHOTS: 1027
- HEADED GOALS: 7
- HAT-TRICKS: 8
- GOALS LEFT: 52
- APPEARANCES: 316
- CONVERSION RATE: 18.8%
- MINUTES PER GOAL: 136

MAJOR CLUB HONOURS

⚽ La Liga: 2015-17 (all Barca) ⚽ Ligue 1: 2018-20, 2022, 2023 ⚽ UEFA Champions League: 2016 (Barca) ⚽ FIFA Club World Cup: 2016 (Barca) ⚽ Copa del Rey: 2015-17 (all Barca) ⚽ Coupe de France: 2018, 2020, 2021

INTERNATIONAL HONOURS

⚽ Copa América: runner-up 2021
⚽ FIFA Confederations Cup: 2013
⚽ Olympic Games: silver medal 2012, gold medal 2016

ACTIVITY AREAS

77

MARCUS RASHFORD

NATIONALITY English
CURRENT CLUB Manchester United

After a couple of quiet seasons, Marcus Rashford is once again back to his best. He prefers to raid from the left side, to be on his stronger right foot, but his pace and heading ability make him just as dangerous in the middle.

BIRTHDATE	31/10/1997
POSITION	FORWARD
HEIGHT	1.80 M
WEIGHT	70 KG
PREFERRED FOOT	RIGHT

- GOALS: 101
- PENALTIES SCORED: 8
- ASSISTS: 41
- GOALS RIGHT: 78
- SHOTS: 686
- HEADED GOALS: 9
- HAT-TRICKS: 1
- GOALS LEFT: 14
- APPEARANCES: 304
- CONVERSION RATE: 14.7%
- MINUTES PER GOAL: 204

MAJOR CLUB HONOURS
- UEFA Europa League: 2017, runner-up 2021
- FA Cup: 2016
- English Football League Cup: 2023

INTERNATIONAL HONOURS
- UEFA European Championship: runner-up 2021
- UEFA Nations League: third place 2019

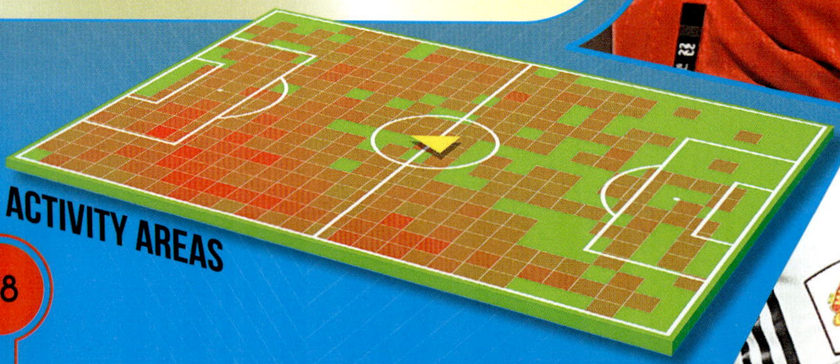

ACTIVITY AREAS

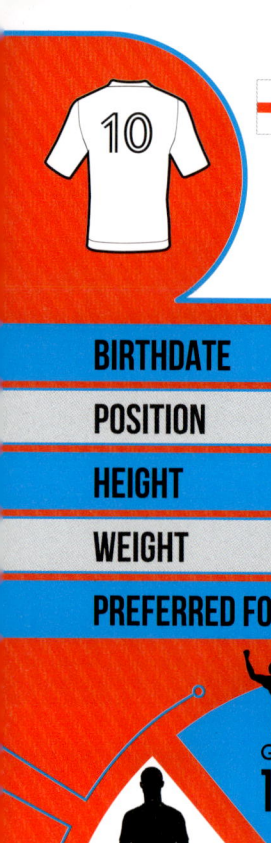

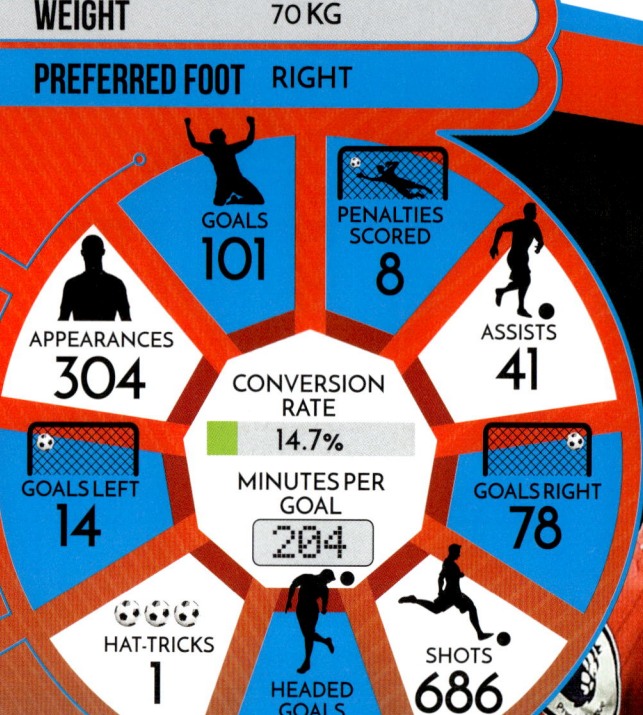

78

MARCO REUS

Marco Reus is an attacker who can lead the front line, play as a second striker or out wide. He is an expert finisher, especially with his right foot, and is also fantastic at setting up chances for his team-mates.

NATIONALITY German

CURRENT CLUB Borussia Dortmund

11

BIRTHDATE	31/05/1989
POSITION	FORWARD
HEIGHT	1.80 M
WEIGHT	71 KG
PREFERRED FOOT	RIGHT

- GOALS: 177
- PENALTIES SCORED: 17
- APPEARANCES: 440
- ASSISTS: 103
- CONVERSION RATE: 16.7%
- MINUTES PER GOAL: 193
- GOALS LEFT: 41
- GOALS RIGHT: 130
- HAT-TRICKS: 3
- HEADED GOALS: 6
- SHOTS: 1060

MAJOR CLUB HONOURS
- Bundesliga: runner-up 2023
- UEFA Champions League: runner-up 2013
- DFB-Pokal: 2017, 2021

INTERNATIONAL HONOURS
- None to date

ACTIVITY AREAS

11

| NATIONALITY | Egyptian |
| CURRENT CLUB | Liverpool |

MOHAMED SALAH

The two-time African Footballer of the Year is a brilliant left-footed attacker who prowls the left wing. Mo Salah has amazing pace with the ability to make angled runs, finding gaps in defences before scoring spectacular goals.

BIRTHDATE	15/06/1992
POSITION	WINGER
HEIGHT	1.75 M
WEIGHT	71 KG
PREFERRED FOOT	LEFT

- GOALS: 223
- PENALTIES SCORED: 25
- ASSISTS: 97
- APPEARANCES: 419
- CONVERSION RATE: 16.9%
- MINUTES PER GOAL: 149
- GOALS LEFT: 180
- GOALS RIGHT: 35
- HAT-TRICKS: 6
- HEADED GOALS: 8
- SHOTS: 1319

MAJOR CLUB HONOURS
⚽ Premier League: 2020 ⚽ UEFA Champions League: 2019, runner-up 2018, runner-up 2022 ⚽ UEFA Super Cup: 2019 ⚽ FIFA Club World Cup: 2019 ⚽ FA Cup: 2022

INTERNATIONAL HONOURS
⚽ CAF Africa Cup of Nations: runner-up 2017, runner-up 2021

ACTIVITY AREAS

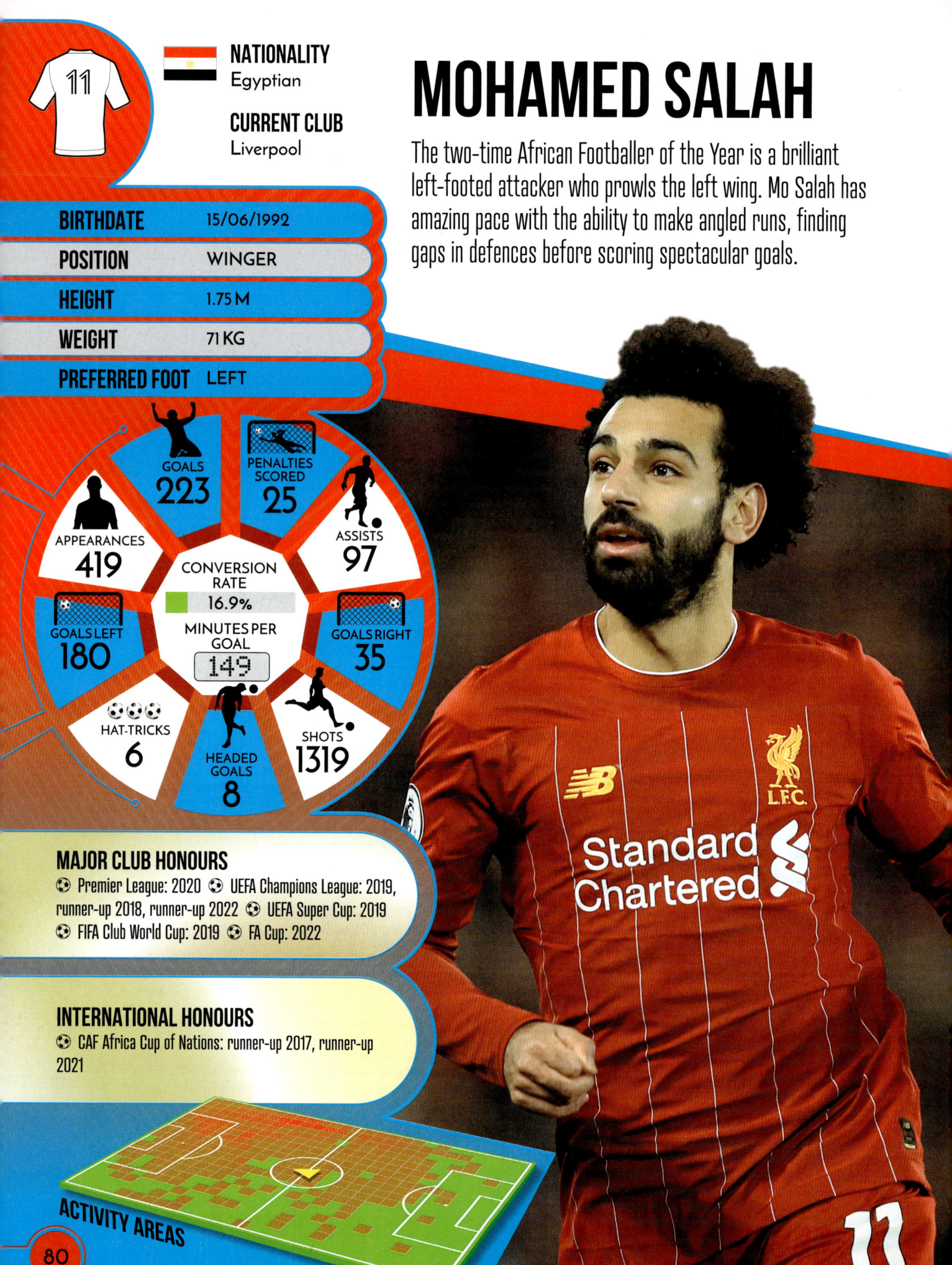

80

SON HEUNG-MIN

Son Heung-Min is at his best when he plays behind the main striker. Although excellent with both feet, attacking from the right side is his strength and he converts a lot of chances that are set up by knock-downs or passes across the box.

NATIONALITY	South Korean
CURRENT CLUB	Tottenham Hotspur
BIRTHDATE	08/07/1992
POSITION	WINGER
HEIGHT	1.84 M
WEIGHT	77 KG
PREFERRED FOOT	BOTH

- GOALS: 169
- PENALTIES SCORED: 1
- ASSISTS: 69
- APPEARANCES: 474
- CONVERSION RATE: 16.4%
- MINUTES PER GOAL: 196
- GOALS LEFT: 67
- GOALS RIGHT: 92
- HAT-TRICKS: 5
- HEADED GOALS: 10
- SHOTS: 1029

MAJOR CLUB HONOURS
- UEFA Champions League: runner-up 2019

INTERNATIONAL HONOURS
- AFC Asian Cup: runner-up 2015

ACTIVITY AREAS

RAHEEM STERLING

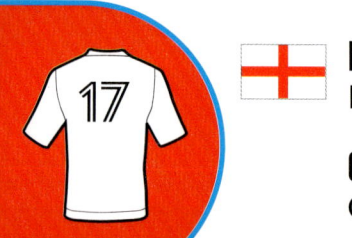

NATIONALITY English
CURRENT CLUB Chelsea

17

The England international's playing-style involves him cutting inside from the left and dribbling past opponents. He also likes to play one-twos with fellow attackers, as well as making runs behind the defensive line to receive a pass that often puts him through on goal.

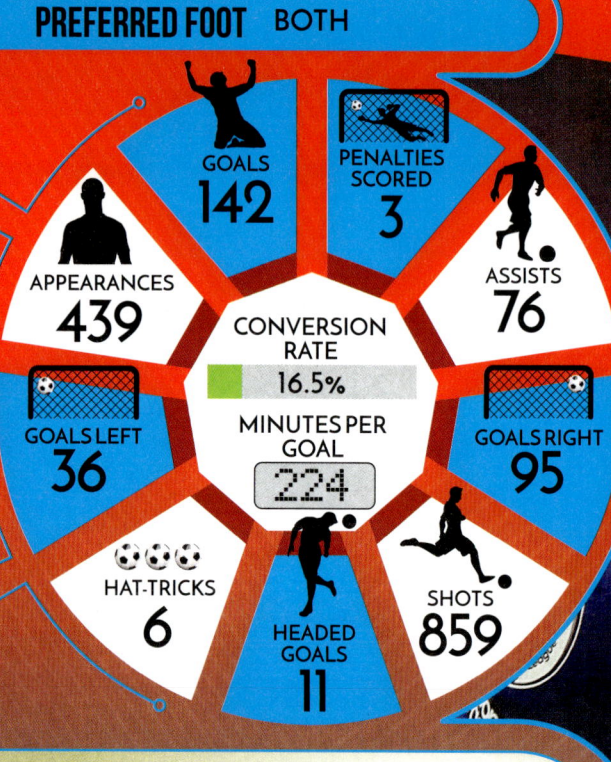

BIRTHDATE	08/12/1994
POSITION	FORWARD
HEIGHT	1.70 M
WEIGHT	69 KG
PREFERRED FOOT	BOTH

- GOALS: 142
- PENALTIES SCORED: 3
- APPEARANCES: 439
- ASSISTS: 76
- CONVERSION RATE: 16.5%
- MINUTES PER GOAL: 224
- GOALS LEFT: 36
- GOALS RIGHT: 95
- HAT-TRICKS: 6
- HEADED GOALS: 11
- SHOTS: 859

MAJOR CLUB HONOURS
- Premier League: 2018, 2019, 2021, 2022 (all Man. City)
- UEFA Champions League: runner-up 2021 (Man. City)
- FA Cup: 2019 (Man. City)

INTERNATIONAL HONOURS
- UEFA European Championship: runner-up 2020
- UEFA Europa Nations League: third place 2019

ACTIVITY AREAS

DUŠAN VLAHOVIĆ

One of world football's most exciting rising stars, Dušan Vlahović is very strong and is great in physical battles. He is excellent in the air, winning headers or flicking the ball on, and almost always converts chances close to goal.

NATIONALITY Serbian

CURRENT CLUB Juventus

BIRTHDATE	28/01/2000
POSITION	STRIKER
HEIGHT	1.90 M
WEIGHT	88 KG
PREFERRED FOOT	LEFT

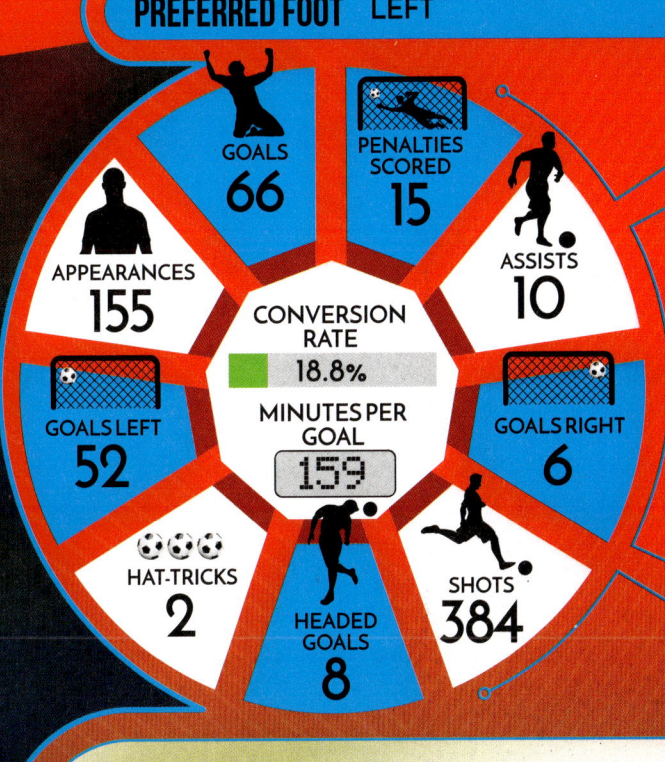

- GOALS: 66
- PENALTIES SCORED: 15
- ASSISTS: 10
- GOALS RIGHT: 6
- SHOTS: 384
- HEADED GOALS: 8
- HAT-TRICKS: 2
- GOALS LEFT: 52
- APPEARANCES: 155
- CONVERSION RATE: 18.8%
- MINUTES PER GOAL: 159

MAJOR CLUB HONOURS
- Serbian SuperLiga: 2017 (Partizan)

INTERNATIONAL HONOURS
- None to date

ACTIVITY AREAS

83

GOALKEEPERS

The goalkeeper is a team's last line of defence and unlike the other positions there is no one playing next to them. There is more pressure on goalkeepers than in any other position because when a keeper makes an error, the chances are that the other team will score. The goalies featured in this section are all great shot-stoppers, but some play outside their penalty areas as sweeper-keepers; others have made their reputation as penalty-savers; then there are those who are great at catching the ball or punching it clear.

WHAT DO THE STATS MEAN?

CATCHES
This is the number of times the keeper has dealt with an attack - usually a cross - by catching the ball.

PENALTIES FACED/SAVED
This is the number of times a goalie has faced a penalty (excludes shoot-outs) and how successful he has been at saving it.

CLEAN SHEETS
Any occasion on which the goalie has not let in a goal for the full duration of the game counts as a clean sheet.

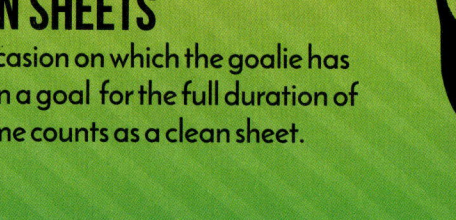

PUNCHES
This is a measure of how often the keeper has dealt with a dangerous ball (usually a cross) by punching it clear.

GOALS CONCEDED
This is the number of goals the keeper has conceded in their career in top-division football.

SAVES
This shows how many times the goalkeeper has stopped a shot or header that was on target.

Did you know?

Goalkeepers can, in theory, score goals with their hands. If they throw a ball downfield and it goes directly into the opposition net, the goal will count but, of course, the ball would have to travel more than 90 metres.

1

NATIONALITY Brazilian
CURRENT CLUB Liverpool

ALISSON

The Brazilian has proved to be a top keeper at Liverpool. Alisson is a superb shot-stopper and great at dealing with crosses. Incredibly quick off his line to foil any threat, he can turn defence into attack by finding team-mates with long or short passes.

BIRTHDATE	02/10/1992
POSITION	GOALKEEPER
HEIGHT	1.93 M
WEIGHT	91 KG
PREFERRED FOOT	RIGHT

- GOALS CONCEDED: 251
- APPEARANCES: 278
- PENALTIES SAVED: 5
- CLEAN SHEETS: 122
- SAVES: 707
- CATCHES: 123
- PENALTIES FACED: 21
- PUNCHES: 108

MAJOR CLUB HONOURS
- Premier League: 2020
- UEFA Champions League: 2019, runner-up 2022
- FIFA Club World Cup: 2019
- FA Cup: 2022

INTERNATIONAL HONOURS
- Copa América: 2019, runner-up 2021

ACTIVITY AREAS

86

BONO

Bono (Yassine Bounou) was born in Canada but represents Morocco, the country where he grew up. Very brave and quick to assess dangerous situations, he cuts down angles very well, is an outstanding shot-stopper and also a great communicator.

NATIONALITY Moroccan
CURRENT CLUB Sevilla

13

BIRTHDATE	05/04/1991
POSITION	GOALKEEPER
HEIGHT	1.95 M
WEIGHT	78 KG
PREFERRED FOOT	RIGHT

- GOALS CONCEDED: 223
- APPEARANCES: 192
- PENALTIES SAVED: 5
- CLEAN SHEETS: 65
- SAVES: 562
- CATCHES: 95
- PENALTIES FACED: 35
- PUNCHES: 72

MAJOR CLUB HONOURS
- UEFA Europa League: 2020, 2023

INTERNATIONAL HONOURS
- None to date

ACTIVITY AREAS

NATIONALITY Belgian

CURRENT CLUB Real Madrid

THIBAUT COURTOIS

Thibaut Courtois uses his height to dominate his penalty area, catching crosses and punching well. An agile shot-stopper, he can get down low to make saves, communicates well with his defence, is excellent coming off his line and passes well.

BIRTHDATE	11/05/1992
POSITION	GOALKEEPER
HEIGHT	1.99 M
WEIGHT	96 KG
PREFERRED FOOT	LEFT

- GOALS CONCEDED: 454
- APPEARANCES: 492
- PENALTIES SAVED: 8
- CLEAN SHEETS: 207
- SAVES: 1238
- CATCHES: 503
- PENALTIES FACED: 44
- PUNCHES: 141

MAJOR CLUB HONOURS
⚽ La Liga: 2014 (Atlét. Mad.), 2020, 2022, runner-up 2023 ⚽ Prem. League: 2015, 2017 (Chelsea) ⚽ UEFA Champs. League: 2022 ⚽ UEFA Europa L: 2012 (Atlét. Mad.) ⚽ FIFA Club World Cup: 2018 ⚽ UEFA Super Cup: 2012 (Atlét Mad) 2022

INTERNATIONAL HONOURS
⚽ FIFA World Cup: third place 2018

ACTIVITY AREAS

DAVID DE GEA

David De Gea is an effective keeper, though unorthodox at times (he is known for using his legs to make saves). Agile and athletic, he marshals his penalty area well. His catching has improved but he is still happier punching the ball the clear.

NATIONALITY Spanish

CURRENT CLUB Manchester United

BIRTHDATE	07/11/1990
POSITION	GOALKEEPER
HEIGHT	1.92 M
WEIGHT	76 KG
PREFERRED FOOT	RIGHT

- GOALS CONCEDED: 637
- APPEARANCES: 568
- PENALTIES SAVED: 9
- CLEAN SHEETS: 191
- SAVES: 1653
- CATCHES: 352
- PENALTIES FACED: 58
- PUNCHES: 186

MAJOR CLUB HONOURS
- Premier League: 2013
- UEFA Europa League: 2010 (Atlético Mad.), 2017, runner-up 2021
- UEFA Super Cup: 2010 (Atlético Mad.)
- FA Cup: 2016, runner-up 2023

INTERNATIONAL HONOURS
- UEFA Nations League: runner-up 2021

ACTIVITY AREAS

89

GIANLUIGI DONNARUMMA

NATIONALITY Italian
CURRENT CLUB Paris Saint-Germain

99

The Italian is an amazing talent who made his Serie A debut aged just 16, won his first Italian cap at 17 and became a European champion at 22. Mentally strong and composed under pressure, he has everything it takes to become an all-time great.

BIRTHDATE	25/02/1999
POSITION	GOALKEEPER
HEIGHT	1.96 M
WEIGHT	90 KG
PREFERRED FOOT	RIGHT

- GOALS CONCEDED: 321
- APPEARANCES: 299
- PENALTIES SAVED: 10
- CLEAN SHEETS: 94
- SAVES: 715
- CATCHES: 191
- PENALTIES FACED: 45
- PUNCHES: 144

MAJOR CLUB HONOURS
- Ligue 1: 2022, 2023
- Supercoppa Italiana: 2016 (AC Milan)

INTERNATIONAL HONOURS
- UEFA European Championship: 2020
- UEFA Nations League: third place 2021, third place 2023

ACTIVITY AREAS

90

EDERSON

Owing to his range of passing and great ball skills, Ederson is often considered a playmaker goalkeeper and counted as one of the best in the English Premier League. He is a fine shot-stopper with a reputation for being a great penalty-kick saver, too.

NATIONALITY Brazilian

CURRENT CLUB Manchester City

31

BIRTHDATE	17/08/1993
POSITION	GOALKEEPER
HEIGHT	1.88 M
WEIGHT	86 KG
PREFERRED FOOT	LEFT

- GOALS CONCEDED: 233
- APPEARANCES: 290
- PENALTIES SAVED: 6
- CLEAN SHEETS: 131
- SAVES: 529
- PENALTIES FACED: 34
- CATCHES: 122
- PUNCHES: 73

MAJOR CLUB HONOURS
- UEFA Champions League: runner-up 2021, 2023
- Premier League: 2018, 2019, 2021, 2022, 2023
- FA Cup: 2019, 2023

INTERNATIONAL HONOURS
- Copa América: 2019, runner-up 2021

ACTIVITY AREAS

PÉTER GULÁCSI

NATIONALITY Hungarian
CURRENT CLUB RB Leipzig

Péter Gulácsi is dedicated to preparing for every football situation he faces. He studies approaching forwards to get an instinct for where they are going to shoot, gets into the right position and then makes difficult saves look very easy.

BIRTHDATE	06/05/1990
POSITION	GOALKEEPER
HEIGHT	1.91 M
WEIGHT	86 KG
PREFERRED FOOT	RIGHT

- GOALS CONCEDED: 320
- APPEARANCES: 264
- PENALTIES SAVED: 3
- CLEAN SHEETS: 78
- SAVES: 634
- PENALTIES FACED: 35
- CATCHES: 154
- PUNCHES: 67

MAJOR CLUB HONOURS
- Austrian Bundesliga: 2014, 2015 (Red Bull Salzburg)
- Austrian Cup: 2014, 2015 (Red Bull Salzburg)
- DFB-Pokal: 2022, 2023

INTERNATIONAL HONOURS
- FIFA U-20 World Cup: third place 2009

ACTIVITY AREAS

SAMIR HANDANOVIĆ

Samir Handanović has awesome positional sense, reaction time, agility, anticipation and athleticism — a combination that makes him an expert between the sticks. He is also a good communicator and defensive organiser.

NATIONALITY
Slovenian

CURRENT CLUB
Inter Milan

BIRTHDATE	14/07/1984
POSITION	GOALKEEPER
HEIGHT	1.93 M
WEIGHT	92 KG
PREFERRED FOOT	RIGHT

GOALS CONCEDED 696
APPEARANCES 636
PENALTIES SAVED 30
CLEAN SHEETS 222
SAVES 1840
PENALTIES FACED 94
CATCHES 578
PUNCHES 294

MAJOR CLUB HONOURS
- Serie A: 2021
- UEFA Champions League: runner-up 2023
- Coppa Italia: 2022, 2023

INTERNATIONAL HONOURS
- None to date

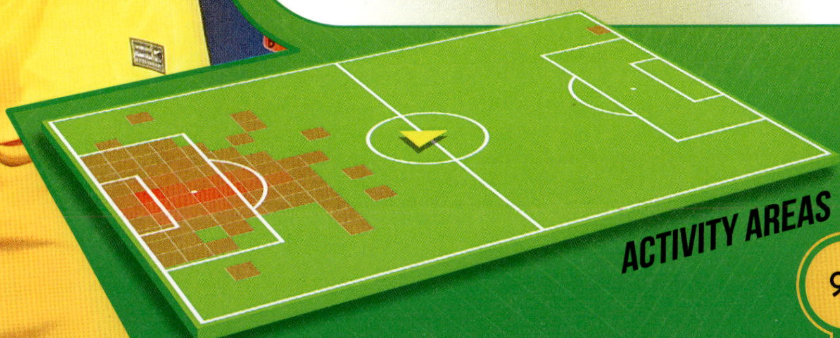

ACTIVITY AREAS

NATIONALITY
French

CURRENT CLUB
Tottenham Hotspur

HUGO LLORIS

Hugo Lloris is a natural leader, good at organising his defence. Armed with excellent reflexes, he is brilliant at coming off his line to clear the danger and then distributing the ball quickly, which has earned him the sweeper-keeper label.

BIRTHDATE	26/12/1986
POSITION	GOALKEEPER
HEIGHT	1.88 M
WEIGHT	82 KG
PREFERRED FOOT	LEFT

- GOALS CONCEDED: 740
- APPEARANCES: 680
- PENALTIES SAVED: 10
- SAVES: 1890
- CLEAN SHEETS: 231
- PENALTIES FACED: 73
- CATCHES: 809
- PUNCHES: 411

MAJOR CLUB HONOURS
- UEFA Champions League: runner-up 2019
- Coupe de France: 2012 (Olympique Lyonnais)

INTERNATIONAL HONOURS
- FIFA World Cup: 2018, runner-up 2022
- UEFA Nations League: 2021
- UEFA European Championship: runner-up 2016

ACTIVITY AREAS

94

EMILIANO MARTÍNEZ

An immensely athletic goalkeeper, Emiliano Martínez is capable of reaching shots going into the top corner with either hand. His quick feet mean he gets into good positions not only to make saves but also reduce the angle for shots.

NATIONALITY
Argentinian

CURRENT CLUB
Aston Villa

BIRTHDATE	02/09/1992
POSITION	GOALKEEPER
HEIGHT	1.95 M
WEIGHT	88 KG
PREFERRED FOOT	RIGHT

- GOALS CONCEDED: 163
- APPEARANCES: 139
- PENALTIES SAVED: 3
- CLEAN SHEETS: 49
- SAVES: 416
- CATCHES: 153
- PENALTIES FACED: 20
- PUNCHES: 20

MAJOR CLUB HONOURS
- FA Cup: 2020 (Arsenal)

INTERNATIONAL HONOURS
- Copa América: 2021
- FIFA World Cup: 2022

ACTIVITY AREAS

16

NATIONALITY
Senegalese

CURRENT CLUB
Chelsea

ÉDOUARD MENDY

French-born Édouard Mendy chose to play for his mother's birthplace Senegal. He is a great shot stopper who dominates his penalty area, marshals his defence and deals with aerial threats with supreme confidence.

BIRTHDATE	01/03/1992
POSITION	GOALKEEPER
HEIGHT	1.94 M
WEIGHT	86 KG
PREFERRED FOOT	RIGHT

GOALS CONCEDED
149

APPEARANCES
164

PENALTIES SAVED
2

CLEAN SHEETS
68

SAVES
375

CATCHES
109

PENALTIES FACED
22

PUNCHES
44

MAJOR CLUB HONOURS
- UEFA Champions League: 2021
- UEFA Super Cup: 2021
- FIFA Club World Cup: 2021

INTERNATIONAL HONOURS
- CAF Africa Cup of Nations: 2021, runner-up 2019

ACTIVITY AREAS

MANUEL NEUER

Manuel Neuer is famous for being football's first sweeper-keeper. He is a fine shot-stopper who commands his penalty area and marshals the defence well. He is also great with the ball at his feet, allowing defenders to play further upfield.

NATIONALITY German

CURRENT CLUB Bayern Munich

BIRTHDATE	27/03/1986
POSITION	GOALKEEPER
HEIGHT	1.93 M
WEIGHT	93 KG
PREFERRED FOOT	RIGHT

- GOALS CONCEDED: 520
- APPEARANCES: 614
- PENALTIES SAVED: 11
- CLEAN SHEETS: 270
- SAVES: 1527
- PENALTIES FACED: 43
- CATCHES: 602
- PUNCHES: 270

MAJOR CLUB HONOURS
- Bundesliga: 2013-2023 (x 11)
- UEFA Champs League: 2013, 2020
- UEFA Super Cup: 2013, 2020
- FIFA Club World Cup: 2013, 2020
- DFB Pokal: 2011 (Schalke 04) 2013-14, 2016, 2019-20

INTERNATIONAL HONOURS
- FIFA World Cup: 2014

ACTIVITY AREAS

NATIONALITY
Slovenian

CURRENT CLUB
Atlético Madrid

JAN OBLAK

One of the world's most accomplished keepers, Jan Oblak is blessed with quick reflexes and agility, and he's excellent at coming off his line and organising his defence. His communication skills make him a reliable team vice-captain.

BIRTHDATE	07/01/1993
POSITION	GOALKEEPER
HEIGHT	1.88 M
WEIGHT	87 KG
PREFERRED FOOT	RIGHT

GOALS CONCEDED: 283
APPEARANCES: 379
PENALTIES SAVED: 9
CLEAN SHEETS: 184
SAVES: 938
PENALTIES FACED: 41
CATCHES: 220
PUNCHES: 103

MAJOR CLUB HONOURS
- La Liga: 2021
- UEFA Champions League: runner-up 2016
- UEFA Europa League: 2018
- UEFA Super Cup: 2018

INTERNATIONAL HONOURS
- None to date

ACTIVITY AREAS

JORDAN PICKFORD

Playing for a struggling team in Everton, Jordan Pickford is kept busy and is an excellent shot-stopper. Not the tallest of goalkeepers, he prefers to punch rather than catch the ball and is also very good at distributing to team-mates.

NATIONALITY English

CURRENT CLUB Everton

BIRTHDATE	07/03/1994
POSITION	GOALKEEPER
HEIGHT	1.85 M
WEIGHT	84 KG
PREFERRED FOOT	LEFT

- GOALS CONCEDED 377
- APPEARANCES 251
- PENALTIES SAVED 5
- CLEAN SHEETS 62
- SAVES 797
- CATCHES 150
- PENALTIES FACED 29
- PUNCHES 133

MAJOR CLUB HONOURS
- None to date

INTERNATIONAL HONOURS
- UEFA European Championship: runner-up 2020
- UEFA Natiom League: third place 2019

ACTIVITY AREAS

99

NICK POPE

22

NATIONALITY English

CURRENT CLUB Newcastle United

Since joining The Magpies, Nick Pope has proved his worth by keeping many clean sheets for his new club. He dominates his penalty area, is excellent at stopping shots, dealing with crosses and being a sweeper-keeper outside the box.

BIRTHDATE	19/04/1992
POSITION	GOALKEEPER
HEIGHT	1.91 M
WEIGHT	76 KG
PREFERRED FOOT	RIGHT

- GOALS CONCEDED: 201
- APPEARANCES: 178
- PENALTIES SAVED: 4
- CLEAN SHEETS: 60
- SAVES: 556
- CATCHES: 203
- PENALTIES FACED: 23
- PUNCHES: 75

MAJOR CLUB HONOURS
- None to date

INTERNATIONAL HONOURS
- None to date

ACTIVITY AREAS

100

KASPER SCHMEICHEL

The son of the legendary keeper Peter Schmeichel, Kasper has many of his father's strengths. He is mentally strong and brilliant in one-on-one situations. He is also superb in the air, commands his penalty area and is a great ball distributor.

NATIONALITY Danish
CURRENT CLUB Nice

BIRTHDATE	05/11/1986
POSITION	GOALKEEPER
HEIGHT	1.89 M
WEIGHT	88 KG
PREFERRED FOOT	RIGHT

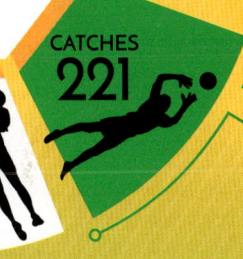

- GOALS CONCEDED: 429
- APPEARANCES: 341
- PENALTIES SAVED: 11
- SAVES: 975
- CLEAN SHEETS: 101
- PENALTIES FACED: 51
- PUNCHES: 130
- CATCHES: 221

MAJOR CLUB HONOURS
- Premier League: 2016 (Leicester City)
- FA Cup: 2021 (Leicester City)

INTERNATIONAL HONOURS
- None to date

ACTIVITY AREAS

101

WOJCIECH SZCZĘSNY

NATIONALITY Polish
CURRENT CLUB Juventus

Wojciech Szczęsny has grown into one of Europe's top-class keepers. A natural shot-stopper with lightning reflexes, he is also great at controlling his penalty area, dealing with crosses and setting up counter-attacks with quick clearances.

BIRTHDATE	18/04/1990
POSITION	GOALKEEPER
HEIGHT	1.95 M
WEIGHT	90 KG
PREFERRED FOOT	RIGHT

- GOALS CONCEDED: 467
- APPEARANCES: 445
- PENALTIES SAVED: 15
- CLEAN SHEETS: 158
- SAVES: 1177
- CATCHES: 365
- PENALTIES FACED: 74
- PUNCHES: 181

MAJOR CLUB HONOURS
⚽ Serie A: 2018, 2019, 2020 ⚽ FA Cup: 2014, 2015 (Arsenal) ⚽ Coppa Italia: 2018, 2021, runner-up 2020, runner-up 2022

INTERNATIONAL HONOURS
⚽ None to date

ACTIVITY AREAS

102

MARC-ANDRÉ TER STEGEN

NATIONALITY
German

CURRENT CLUB
Barcelona

A brilliant sweeper-keeper, Marc-André ter Stegen is simply world class. In addition to his fine goalkeeping qualities, he is exceptional at anticipating opponents who have beaten the offside trap, and can rush off his line to meet the danger.

BIRTHDATE	30/04/1992
POSITION	GOALKEEPER
HEIGHT	1.87 M
WEIGHT	85 KG
PREFERRED FOOT	RIGHT

GOALS CONCEDED 447
APPEARANCES 454
PENALTIES SAVED 7
CLEAN SHEETS 182
SAVES 1264
CATCHES 456
PENALTIES FACED 46
PUNCHES 192

MAJOR CLUB HONOURS
⚽ La Liga: 2015, 2016, 2018, 2019, 2023 ⚽ UEFA Champions League: 2015 ⚽ UEFA Super Cup: 2015 ⚽ FIFA Club World Cup: 2015 ⚽ Copa del Rey: 2015, 2016, 2017, 2018, 2021

INTERNATIONAL HONOURS
⚽ FIFA Confederations Cup: 2017

ACTIVITY AREAS

MANAGERS

Head coaches are as different to each other as players who play in different positions. But the majority of the 12 featured in this section have one thing in common: they are all winners, either in their domestic leagues or in continental competitions. Some, such as Laurent Blanc (opposite), were legendary players in their own right and title winners well before they entered management, while others, such as Liverpool boss Jürgen Klopp, did little on the field but have had great success as the brains behind a top side.

WHAT DO THE STATS MEAN?

GAMES MANAGED
This is the number of matches the coach has been in charge of across their career in top-flight football.

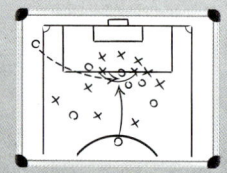

TEAMS MANAGED
The number of clubs (first teams only) that the coach has managed during their career to date.

WINS
This is the number of games the coach has won, including one leg of a cup-tie, even if the tie was lost on aggregate or penalties.

TROPHIES
The trophy list features the head coach's success in domestic top divisions, national and league cups and international club competitions, except any super cups.

Did you know?

As a manager, Laurent Blanc rarely takes part in training sessions but rather takes a step back – leaving the technical aspects to his assistants. Instead, he focuses on the players in individual interviews.

CARLO ANCELOTTI

Formerly an international player, Carlo Ancelotti uses different systems depending on the opposition and players available. His favourite formation is 4—4—2, sometimes in a diamond, other times with four midfielders in a line across the pitch.

NATIONALITY
Italian

CURRENT CLUB
Real Madrid

YEARS AS HEAD COACH: 28
FIRST CLUB: REGGIANA

CLUBS MANAGED	GAMES	LEAGUE TITLES
10	1284	5

WINS	DRAW	LOSSES
756	287	241

CHAMPIONS LEAGUE TROPHIES	EUROPA LEAGUE TROPHIES	OTHER TROPHIES*
4	0	8

*Excludes Super Cups

MAJOR CLUB HONOURS
- La Liga: 2022, runner-up 2023
- UEFA Champions League: 2003, 2007 (all AC Milan), 2014, 2022
- FIFA Club World Cup: 2007 (AC Milan), 2014, 2022
- UEFA Super Cup: 1993, 2007 (all AC Milan), 2014, 2022
- Serie A: 2004 (AC Milan)
- Premier League: 2010 (Chelsea)
- Ligue 1: 2013 (Paris St Germain)
- Copa del Rey: 2014, 2023
- Bundesliga: 2017 (Bayern Munich)

LAURENT BLANC

Laurent Blanc has a track record of coaching success in Ligue 1, having been a big-time winner as a player. His coaching policy focuses on being solid in defence and ensuring his players are comfortable in possession of the ball.

NATIONALITY
French

CURRENT CLUB
Olympique Lyonnais

YEARS AS HEAD COACH: 16
FIRST CLUB: BORDEAUX

CLUBS MANAGED	GAMES	LEAGUE TITLES
5	447	4

WINS	DRAW	LOSSES
272	87	88

CHAMPIONS LEAGUE TROPHIES	EUROPA LEAGUE TROPHIES	OTHER TROPHIES*
0	0	6

*Excludes Super Cups

MAJOR CLUB HONOURS
- Ligue 1: 2009 (Bordeaux), 2014, 2015, 2016 (Paris Saint-Germain)
- Coupe de France: 2015, 2016 (Paris Saint-Germain)

ANTONIO CONTE

Although Antonio Conte varies his tactics and formations, they are always based on a strong defence, so his teams tend to be great counter-attackers. Always animated on the touchline, he instils a great team spirit into his side.

NATIONALITY: Italian

CURRENT CLUB: Free agent

YEARS AS HEAD COACH: 17

FIRST CLUB: AREZZO

CLUBS MANAGED: 9
GAMES: 587
LEAGUE TITLES: 5
WINS: 342
DRAW: 136
LOSSES: 109
CHAMPIONS LEAGUE TROPHIES: 0
EUROPA LEAGUE TROPHIES: 0
OTHER TROPHIES*: 2

MAJOR CLUB HONOURS
- Serie A: 2012, 2013, 2014 (all Juventus), 2021 (Internazionale)
- Premier League: 2017 (Chelsea)
- FA Cup: 2018 (Chelsea)
- UEFA Europa League: runner-up 2020 (Inter Milan)

*Excludes Super Cups

UNAI EMERY

Unai Emery has enjoyed great success managing clubs that have a modest budget. His preference is either a 4–2–3–1 formation or 4–4–2, the choice dependent on the attacking skills of the two central midfielders and their ability to retain possession.

NATIONALITY: Spanish

CURRENT CLUB: Aston Villa

YEARS AS HEAD COACH: 19

FIRST CLUB: LORCA DEPORTIVA

CLUBS MANAGED: 9
GAMES: 953
LEAGUE TITLES: 1
WINS: 508
DRAW: 210
LOSSES: 235
CHAMPIONS LEAGUE TROPHIES: 0
EUROPA LEAGUE TROPHIES: 4
OTHER TROPHIES*: 4

MAJOR CLUB HONOURS
- UEFA Europa League: 2014, 2015, 2016 (all Sevilla), 2021 (Villareal), runner-up 2019 (Arsenal)
- Ligue 1: 2018 (Paris Saint-Germain)
- Coupe de France: 2017, 2018 (all Paris Saint-Germain)

*Excludes Super Cups

CHRISTOPHE GALTIER

Christophe Galtier builds his teams from the back and is happy to go with either 4–2–3–1 or 4–3–3 formations. He made his reputation as a coach who got teams out of relegation trouble with excellent organisation on the pitch.

NATIONALITY: French
CURRENT CLUB: Paris Saint-Germain
YEARS AS HEAD COACH: 14
FIRST CLUB: SAINT-ETIENNE

CLUBS MANAGED: 4
GAMES: 606
LEAGUE TITLES: 2
WINS: 282
DRAW: 155
LOSSES: 169
CHAMPIONS LEAGUE TROPHIES: 0
EUROPA LEAGUE TROPHIES: 0
OTHER TROPHIES*: 1

MAJOR CLUB HONOURS
- Ligue 1: 2021 (Lille), 2023
- Coupe de France: runner-up (Nice)

*Excludes Super Cups

PEP GUARDIOLA

Once a great midfielder himself, Pep Guardiola devised the *tika-taka* passing system at Barcelona (2008–12). Disciplined in possession, without the ball his teams press the opposition into making mistakes and then launch rapid counter-attacks.

NATIONALITY: Spanish
CURRENT CLUB: Manchester City
YEARS AS HEAD COACH: 15
FIRST CLUB: BARCELONA

CLUBS MANAGED: 3
GAMES: 821
LEAGUE TITLES: 11
WINS: 600
DRAW: 123
LOSSES: 98
CHAMPIONS LEAGUE TROPHIES: 3
EUROPA LEAGUE TROPHIES: 0
OTHER TROPHIES*: 13

MAJOR CLUB HONOURS
- UEFA Champions League: 2009, 2011 (Barcelona), runner-up 2021, 2023
- UEFA Super Cup: 2009, 2011 (Barcelona), 2013 (B. Munich)
- FIFA Club World Cup: 2009, 2011 (Barcelona), 2013 (B. Munich)
- La Liga: 2009, 2010, 2011 (Barcelona)
- Bundesliga: 2014, 2015, 2016 (B. Munich)
- Premier League: 2018, 2019, 2021, 2022, 2023
- FA Cup: 2019, 2023

*Excludes Super Cups

JÜRGEN KLOPP

Jürgen Klopp brings great enthusiasm to the technical area and expects his team to show a similar spirit. His team are strong defensively, try to win back the ball immediately after they lose it and counter-attack at great speed.

NATIONALITY: German
CURRENT CLUB: Liverpool
YEARS AS HEAD COACH: 22
FIRST CLUB: MAINZ 05

CLUBS MANAGED	GAMES	LEAGUE TITLES
3	1022	3

WINS	DRAW	LOSSES
549	245	228

CHAMPIONS LEAGUE TROPHIES	EUROPA LEAGUE TROPHIES	OTHER TROPHIES*
1	0	4

MAJOR CLUB HONOURS
- UEFA Champions League: runner-up 2013 (B. Dortmund), runner-up 2018, 2019, runner-up 2022
- UEFA Super Cup: 2019
- FIFA Club World Cup: 2019
- Bundesliga: 2011, 2012 (all B. Dortmund)
- DFB-Pokal: 2012 (B. Dortmund)
- Premier League: 2020
- FA Cup: 2022

*Excludes Super Cups

JULEN LOPETEGUI

Julen Lopetegui likes his teams to be creative in attack and wants his full-backs to give width, dragging defenders out of position and then filling the gaps they leave behind. He preaches a never give up attitude from his teams.

NATIONALITY: Spanish
CURRENT CLUB: Wolverhampton Wanderers
YEARS AS HEAD COACH: 20
FIRST CLUB: RAYO VALLECANO

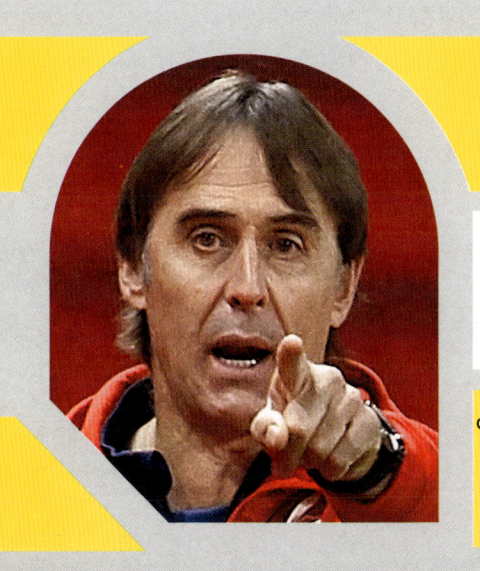

CLUBS MANAGED	GAMES	LEAGUE TITLES
6	338	0

WINS	DRAW	LOSSES
178	80	80

CHAMPIONS LEAGUE TROPHIES	EUROPA LEAGUE TROPHIES	OTHER TROPHIES*
0	1	0

MAJOR CLUB HONOURS
- UEFA Europa League: 2020 (Sevilla)
- UEFA Super Cup: runner-up 2020 (Sevilla)
- UEFA Super Cup: runner-up 2018 (Real Madrid)

*Excludes Super Cups

JOSÉ MOURINHO

José Mourinho focuses his team strength on midfield, normally with a player in front of the defence and two or three further upfield. He expects his defenders to be tactically and technically excellent, and tends to pick experienced players.

NATIONALITY
Portuguese

CURRENT CLUB
AS Roma

YEARS AS HEAD COACH: 23

FIRST CLUB: BENFICA

CLUBS MANAGED: 10
GAMES: 1105
LEAGUE TITLES: 8
WINS: 688
DRAW: 230
LOSSES: 187
CHAMPIONS LEAGUE TROPHIES: 2
EUROPA LEAGUE TROPHIES: 2
OTHER TROPHIES*: 9

*Excludes Super Cups

MAJOR CLUB HONOURS
- UEFA Champions League: 2004 (Porto), 2010 (Inter Milan)
- UEFA Europa League: 2017 (Man Utd), runner-up 2023
- UEFA Cup: 2003 (Porto)
- Premier League: 2005, 2006, 2015 (all Chelsea)
- FA Cup: 2007 (Chelsea)
- Serie A: 2009, 2010 (all Inter Milan)
- Coppa Italia: 2010 (Inter Milan)
- La Liga: 2012 (Real Madrid)
- Copa del Rey: 2011 (Real Madrid)
- UEFA Europa Conf. League: 2022

THOMAS TUCHEL

Thomas Tuchel has won multiple trophies. He is flexible, changing tactics to suit the players he has available, and a strong believer in *Gegenpressing*, immediately trying to regain possession instead of dropping into a more defensive mode.

NATIONALITY
German

CURRENT CLUB
Bayern Munich

YEARS AS HEAD COACH: 16

FIRST CLUB: FC AUGSBURG II

CLUBS MANAGED: 6
GAMES: 529
LEAGUE TITLES: 3
WINS: 300
DRAW: 108
LOSSES: 121
CHAMPIONS LEAGUE TROPHIES: 1
EUROPA LEAGUE TROPHIES: 0
OTHER TROPHIES*: 4

*Excludes Super Cups

MAJOR CLUB HONOURS
- Bundesliga: 2023
- UEFA Champions League: 2021 (Chelsea), runner-up 2020 (PSG)
- FIFA World Club Cup: 2021 (Chelsea)
- UEFA Super Cup: 2021 (Chelsea)
- Ligue 1: 2019, 2020 (all PSG)
- Coupe de France: 2020 (PSG)
- Trophée des Champions: 2018, 2019 (all PSG)
- DfB Pokal: 2017 (Borussia Dortmund)
- Coupe de la Ligue: 2020 (PSG)

STEFANO PIOLI

Stefano Pioli is superb at instilling confidence into his players. This is partly because he is flexible with his tactics and focuses more on the management of the individuals, getting the best out of them on the pitch. He favours a 4–2–3–1 formation.

NATIONALITY Italian

CURRENT CLUB AC Milan

YEARS AS HEAD COACH: 20

FIRST CLUB: SALERNITANA

CLUBS MANAGED	GAMES	LEAGUE TITLES
13	819	1

WINS	DRAW	LOSSES
336	239	244

CHAMPIONS LEAGUE TROPHIES	EUROPA LEAGUE TROPHIES	OTHER TROPHIES*
0	0	0

MAJOR CLUB HONOURS
- Serie A: 2022

*Excludes Super Cups

DIEGO SIMEONE

Diego Simeone likes to use a formation which is almost a 4–2–2–2 unit, with wide midfielders playing between the two central ones and the strikers. Strong defensively, his teams are great at defending set pieces and dangerous in attack.

NATIONALITY Argentinian

CURRENT CLUB Atlético Madrid

YEARS AS HEAD COACH: 17

FIRST CLUB: RACING CLUB

CLUBS MANAGED	GAMES	LEAGUE TITLES
6	834	4

WINS	DRAW	LOSSES
465	198	171

CHAMPIONS LEAGUE TROPHIES	EUROPA LEAGUE TROPHIES	OTHER TROPHIES*
0	2	1

MAJOR CLUB HONOURS
- UEFA Champions League: runner-up 2014, 2016
- UEFA Europa League: 2012, 2018
- UEFA Super Cup: 2012, 2018
- La Liga: 2014, 2021
- Copa del Rey: 2013
- Primera División Apertura 2006 (Estudiantes)
- Primera División Clausura 2008 (Racing Club)

NOTES